Dan

Fine
Bool
Bool
pers

To re

25.

O

Why Women Lose at Bridge

Have you ever wondered why women do not achieve more wins at the top level in the field of championship bridge? The game is a mental exercise rather than a physical one, after all, and it is hard to see why women should not do as well as men.

Australian authoress Joyce Nicholson sought an answer to the problem by sending a questionnaire to the members of the International Bridge Press Association—the top writers on the game, both male and female. This book is the result.

Are women really too emotional, remarkably illogical and unable to concentrate for any length of time? Do they lack aggression, competitive spirit and the will to win? Do you perhaps believe women are sensible and spend more time than men on the important things in life? And how far does sex, as distinct from gender, come into the picture?

Whatever your views on the subject of women and bridge, whether you are male or female, a keen player or a non-player, a fierce feminist or an ardent anti-feminist, you are sure to be stimulated by the ideas expressed in this original book.

Why Women Lose at Bridge

JOYCE NICHOLSON

LONDON
VICTOR GOLLANCZ LTD
in association with Peter Crawley
1985

First published in Great Britain 1985
by Victor Gollancz Ltd,
14 Henrietta Street, London WC2E 8QJ

British Library Cataloguing in Publication Data
Nicholson, Joyce
   Why women lose at bridge.—(Master bridge series)
   1. Women contract bridge players
   I. Title   II. Series
   795.41′5′088042   GV1282.32

   ISBN 0-575-03709-1
   ISBN 0-575-03721-0 Pbk

Photoset and printed in Great Britain by
Photobooks (Bristol) Ltd

Contents

Foreword

by Hugh Kelsey

It is my pleasure and my privilege to introduce a book that is unique in bridge literature—a serious and sensitive study of the reasons why women do not have greater success in the harsh, competitive field of championship bridge.

The author is an Australian writer, editor and publisher who was converted to feminism in middle life and to bridge a little later. She conceived the idea of sending a questionnaire to all members of the International Bridge Press Association, inviting their views on a number of aspects of women's bridge. The book is based on the answers received from these top writers, both male and female, and the author's interpretation of the answers.

There is no doubt that the odds are stacked against women in what is predominantly a man's world. Women who seek pre-eminence at bridge are disadvantaged in a number of ways, just as they are in other fields of endeavour. Apart from the 'sex-role conditioning' that women experience from the cradle onwards, family and financial ties often make it difficult for them to accord the game the single-minded commitment that is so necessary for advancement.

Not all readers will agree with everything the author has to say on the subject. Hackles are sure to be raised in some quarters by the lack of emphasis on the biological factors that make men and women suited to different roles. But readers of both sexes, feminist and anti-feminist, will be stimulated by this full and frank discussion of a subject that has hitherto been kept under wraps.

Why do the top men players seldom choose top women as their partners for important events? My own case is fairly typical. Ideally, I would like to choose my partners according to their ability, without regard to their sex. But this is not an ideal world. If I seldom play with women it is mainly (a) in the interests of marital harmony (my wife is a non-player), and (b) because few women of the required ability live within range. Both these reasons, and many others, are discussed in this book.

I firmly believe that a woman's brain is in no way inferior to a man's. There is no intrinsic reason why women should not excel in what is mainly a cerebral activity. On the few occasions that I have played in mixed pairs I have been impressed by some of the winning decisions made by my partners. Often these have smacked of feminine intuition or flair, but, as I wrote in one of my books: 'The real secret of the expert is the ability to make logic seem like flair.' A woman's logic may be heavily disguised, but it is no less valid or less effective on that account.

Over the years there have been some women who were demonstrably the equals of the top men. Josephine Culbertson, Helen Sobel and Rixi Markus are names that spring to mind. And women have enjoyed a number of recent successes. The Dutch women's team entered the open trials in 1984 and came close as a whisker to winning. And in the same year the team that won the Gold Cup, Britain's premier team event, contained three women.

The question of why men are usually selected as non-playing captains of women's teams is a puzzling one, and it is interesting to speculate on reactions if a woman were to be appointed as captain of a men's team. To the best of my knowledge this has never happened, nor is it likely to happen. I captained the British women's team in the 1984 Olympiad and found it a worthwhile experience. All the members of the team played aggressive, competitive bridge, accepted my decisions without question, and showed no signs of the emotional or temperamental problems that some of the answers to the questionnaire might lead one to expect.

Members of a team need to be able to get on well with their captain and they must also respect his or her bridge ability and judgment. There is no reason why a woman should not do the job, and indeed there have been many successful woman captains. But for every woman with the right qualifications there are ten men, and I suspect this is the only reason why men are so often chosen.

Many other fascinating aspects of women's bridge are discussed by Joyce Nicholson in this unusual book, and I propose to keep you from your enjoyment of it no longer.

CHAPTER 1

Hooked

I have a confession to make. About my age. It was only seven years ago, at the age of 58, that I played my first game of contract bridge and two months later I played my first game of duplicate. But that night I knew I was hooked. 'Take a good look at me,' I felt like saying to everyone at the club, where I knew no one but my partner, 'for I'm going to be around a long time. I am here to stay.' I was another victim of this all-absorbing, fascinating, obsessional game. To quote the famous Alan Sontag, bridge is 'the most intellectually demanding and rewarding sport on earth . . . one of the most complex and devilish games the human race has managed to devise.'

I did play some bridge when I was young. My first introduction to it was an example of the way parents view differently the education of their sons and their daughters. Whereas my mother would sit beside my brother and help him with his homework, and both my parents encouraged him to go to the university, my father used to urge me, at the age of nine, to 'stop studying. Come and make up a four at bridge.' That was in 1928, and it was auction bridge I learned. The family never played contract. In fact, in my stupidity and innocence, I always thought it a completely different game.

In those years, from 1928 to 1931, my father wrote and published several little booklets on bridge, under the pseudonym Ace High. In retrospect he appeared to lose interest in the game, with his unwillingness for detail, when conventions became fashionable. His last book was called *Contract Without Conventions* (1931, 1/- or 20c.). One wonders what he would have made of bridge today, with a forcing pass system! Whatever the reason, bridge stopped in our house around 1931, and my knowledge of it also ceased for another 45 years. When I returned to the fold, the first thing was to unlearn what I knew. All those rules my father had drummed into me such as 'lead the highest of your partner's suit', 'lead the top of touching honours', assessing one's hand by counting 'quick tricks' had to be abandoned.

During that 45 years' absence from bridge I became publisher, author, wife and mother, but I made many bad decisions. I left school too early, married too young and had too many children. Although I loved my children, I came to hate the mothering role. I regretted my lack of proper academic education. I resented my financial dependence. I fought this by writing books at home, and I never lost my love of cards. During those years of domesticity, I spent hours playing with the children everything from Strip-Jack-Naked, Donkey, Please and Thankyou, through Poker, Black-jack, to Solo. I even wrote a book, *How to Play Solo*, way back in 1950, using my father's pseudonym, believing that no one would buy a book on cards written by a woman. That book still sells about 5000 copies a year. But I never played bridge. Because of my peculiar misunderstanding about the difference between auction and contract (a certain dumbness in my make-up) if any adult group asked me to play 'contract bridge', I would reply that I did not know how. I always wished I had time to learn.

And all those years I was plagued with guilt because I sought these other outlets, I was not content to be a wife and mother.

Then, in 1972, my life changed. I started reading feminist

12

literature. I discovered there was no good reason why I, because I was born female, should enjoy the traditional female roles. I had been programmed to lead a life for which I was not necessarily suited. I began to think for myself and actually to make some good decisions. I returned to full-time, well-paid work. I became more confident. I commenced doing what *I* wanted to do, not what other people wanted me to do. I found it was no longer possible to be a supportive, loving wife, spending countless hours on activities I did not enjoy. So I left my husband, and now live alone, loving it.

Then came another good decision. Someone asked me to a bridge party. Not again did I say I did not know how to play. I bought a short Goren how-to book and had the audacity to go along, never having played contract bridge before. You know the rest, and life continues to get better.

As most readers also know, bridge players fall into two categories. Those who become obsessed by the game, who look upon it as a way of life, and those who play it as a more intelligent way of passing their spare time. Given my nature, it was inevitable that I would join the ranks of the obsessed. Of course, one-half of me was sorry I had not started much younger. Instead of spending all those years being an unwilling wife and mother and a mediocre writer, I could have been a business person and a bridge player and doubtless a better one. But my other half disagreed. I came to observe that many good and experienced players were far inferior to the best. Perhaps I too would never have progressed beyond a certain point, and what better new interest could be found at the age of 60? What more fascinating skill could be pursued in old age?

For the uninitiated, there are two reasons why bridge is endlessly fascinating. There is no conquering it. No matter how much one improves, no matter how hard one works at it, there are new heights to scale, new layers to unfold, new dimensions to discover. It endlessly renews itself, not only within one's own perceptions of it, and skill at it, but in the ever-changing nature of the game. Just as my father complained of simple conventions back in 1931, so do many of today's top players complain of multi-two openings, forcing pass systems, obscure doubles, etc. No other game produces the endless variations that bridge does.

The other unique feature of it is that the novice can not only play against the top players, but can win the occasional good score. Imagine if the enthusiastic club tennis player could not only play against John McEnroe or Jimmy Connors, but could win a game from one of them. Most of us would never win one point. Most of us never get near enough even to touch the greats in any other game or sport, let alone play against them. In bridge you not only sit down at the same table and play against them, you occasionally get a good score. I managed one great score against the celebrated Italian player Benito Garozzo in Biarritz. There's nothing unusual about it. There's quite a bit of luck in bridge. The good players win in the end, of course, the same ones repeatedly. Luck does not continue, but what a stimulating dimension this sort of experience adds to bridge.

So the more I played, the more enthralling and exciting it became. I found myself playing practically every night, many weekends, all my holidays. One thing only became depressing. As congress followed congress, and one studied those who qualified for the finals, it was only too obvious that the majority were men. Yet three-quarters of those playing were women, and there did not seem any good reason for men's ascendancy in what was surely a mental activity. Women's brains are as good as men's. Some women consistently prove they can gain top places in examinations at all levels in all subjects, including maths and sciences. For all this, there are very good reasons why so few of them ever reach the top in any area of endeavour.

One wonders at the number of articles written stating that

14

only 17% of top management are women, or only 23% are heads of schools, or only a small per cent top surgeons, or judges, or whatever. What is amazing, considering the obstacles, is that any women get to the top, anywhere. What are the obstacles?

Firstly, most girls are reared from birth, by their toys, their stories, their schools, their parents, their peers and the media, to be non-competitive, non-aggressive, sweet, passive, lady-like, supportive, unselfish, to be in fact mothers and wives. If they are too tough, rough or clever, the young man will not like them enough to date them or marry them. Jessie Bernard in *The Future of Marriage*[1] points out that even within marriages, for career women to be happily married their careers have to be less important than their husbands. They must be less clever. Most young women believe their future happiness lies in being a successful wife or mother. That is of prime importance, so most young women behave and act to achieve that role. This takes most of them out of the work force for a long while, if not forever, so naturally they do not get to the top.

I was a perfect example of this. I had a wonderful father, and we were great friends. We went hiking, camping, to watch and play sport. Above all, he and I worked together. I started at the age of 12, after school and during my school holidays, to help in his small publishing business. I loved it. I learned about editing, design, typography, paste-up, typing, accounting, running a small business. Then, believing that education was not important for girls—for would I not get married?—my parents encouraged me to leave school at 15, and work full-time. At the same time, they made many sacrifices to send my brother to university. Then, after nine years, I left for full-time domesticity. Although I knew all about my father's business, and had regularly managed it in his absence, there was no thought by myself, my parents or my peers, that I would continue working in it. I was assuredly

15

not going to reach the top of my career. I gave it up. I opted for marriage and motherhood.

Secondly, even if women go back into the work force quite quickly, they still lose several years on the promotion ladder or several years of keeping up-to-date with new research and new trends in their field.

Thirdly, those women who keep working while having their children, or return immediately, are faced with the two-job syndrome, running their home and their paid work. This is a double burden, which physically handicaps and wearies women, and also takes up the extra time the successful man needs to reach the top.

Fourthly, the few women who do not get married or have children, or who are 'superwoman' enough to manage home and job satisfactorily, still face male prejudices. Most promotions and appointments are made by men, and usually men are selected. Stories are legion of men passing over women for a new job, a promotion, or a training course, in case she 'gets married' or 'becomes pregnant'. The strange thing is that few ambitious young men stay long in one business or company, and after the promotion or the special training, the company loses them.

Finally, because the strain of combining two jobs is so great, many women find it not worth their while to make the effort. They settle for the second-class job of being a full-time wife and mother, they devote their many skills to their husbands and children. A full-time housewife is not a second-class job, but no matter how much men may protest to the contrary, that is how they consider it.

Indeed, in becoming a full-time wife and mother, because the skills she had are lessened or lost, a woman often does appear second rate. To quote from one leading bridge writer, 'Men are better at bridge because they are better at everything'. That is what many people believe, but it is only partly true. Many women are quite as good at cooking as leading chefs, but this skill is confined to their family and friends. The same principle applies to sewing and many other crafts. The family benefits. The woman suffers by appearing a lesser person, she is not paid for her skills, she loses status and power, and in many cases she does lose the paid skills she had.

To return to women and bridge, the problem was that these five obstacles did not seem to apply to bridge, a cerebral game of skill. Women even seemed to have some advantages. While their children are babies, they can keep their knowledge of bridge up-to-date by reading. Once their children are older, they often have more spare time than their husbands. If they work outside the home, it is usually part-time and/or, because women generally fill lower positions, less demanding. Admittedly, if they do not work, they will be dependent financially on their husbands agreeing to pay their bridge expenses. Many will be lost to bridge. But many husbands and wives spend about the same time on the game, and still the men generally perform the better. Finally, men's attitudes do not seem to discriminate against women. In the leading bridge-playing countries, most places in teams are gained through trials. Selection does not occur.

These were the random thoughts that wandered through my mind. There did not seem any positive or strong reasons why women did not win as much at bridge as men.

CHAPTER 2

It Started in Biarritz

Then came Biarritz. Biarritz was the venue for the World Championships in 1982, an event held only every four years, at which accredited pairs and teams from countries all round the world can compete. This is in contrast to most international events, where only one team represents their country, and only certain countries qualify to compete.

I was fortunate enough to be able to play there in both the mixed and the open pairs, and suddenly the subject of women bridge players presented itself again and became not only a serious one, but one worthy of study. Some clues even began to emerge. It resembled a detective story.

It was a wonderful experience, playing against the world's greats, but two things immediately became apparent. As the pairs came to one's table, and one surreptitiously studied their system cards to catch a famous name, it was obvious that, *generally speaking*, the big-name men players treated the mixed in a much lighter manner than the open. They joked. They chatted. In the open they were deadly, inexorably serious. (Ah! Male attitudes, thought I!)

I also noticed that, *generally speaking*, women did not take their game as seriously. The finals in the Open and Women's were played concurrently, and there was not the same atmosphere in the Women's as in the Open. For example, I, with several others, kibitzed (watched) Wolff and Hamman in the finals, but there were few people kibitzing the women players. The Women's finished long before the Open. The

18

atmosphere at the Women's tables was less tense, they appeared to grumble more, to take their losses more lightly, and when a bad run started, to lose interest.

When the pairs events were finished and the Rosenblum Knockout Teams commenced, in which I was not playing, along came another of those half-accidental good decisions. Assiduously studying the Daily Bulletin each morning, I found a paragraph appealing for more people to join the International Bridge Press Association. As a publisher and small-time reviewer of bridge books, I was eligible. Why not? I intended kibitzing one of the Australian teams, but this left plenty of time. Dreams of spending it on the beach were fading. It looked as if it was going to rain every day (it did), so here was a good opportunity to learn more about the bridge world.

So that day I wandered along to the press office, presided over by that marvellous duo, the Ducheynes, and put in my application. What another life-changing decision. Firstly, because of the great numbers, most kibitzers were not allowed to watch the teams. There was space only for the press—if one could find a chair. I arrived early each morning, and once a chair was found, carried it around more possessively than my handbag. Thus I was able to kibitz every hand of the teams event, or, more specifically, those of my professional partner, Paul Lavings.

My initiation into bridge had involved, as with all beginners, a battle to acquire better players as partners. Having started at such an advanced age, this was particularly difficult. It took me three years, another indication of a terrible dumbness, to make the amazing discovery that one could pay good players to partner one. This not only improved one's bridge, but resulted in better scores. By chance, in Sydney in July 1982, Paul, who has eight times represented Australia in international teams and ranks fifth highest in total masterpoints in Australia, was available for the mixed. After what was a very inauspicious beginning, we

19

made an arrangement that when he was not playing in big events, important for selection, he would play with me. This involved learning his Transfer Precision system. So, with my all-important press pass, to be able to kibitz every card he played at Biarritz was not only a great experience, but hopefully educational. At Biarritz, he also introduced me to brown rice. But that is another story.

The second bonus from joining the IBPA was that, even with kibitzing, there was still plenty of spare time, and I spent some of this in the press room, and naturally talked with many of the journalists about the various events and bridge generally. At some stage the subject of women players was mentioned.

'Why do you think women are not as good at bridge?' I asked.

'They are not aggressive enough,' said a Belgian journalist. Not aggressive? I was amazed. What had aggression to do with bridge? Aggression meant men being angry, fighting, making wars. Of course women were not aggressive. We've been taught from birth to be passive, patient, feminine, loving, clean, co-operative. That is a woman's role. Patience and love are the characteristics of a good wife and mother, not aggression.

I asked someone else.

'Women are not aggressive enough,' he said. 'They don't compete enough in the bidding. They don't make aggressive leads. They play too passively.'

Suddenly, a whole new world of bridge-playing opened up, and I had the first hints of an answer to my problem. I had been too busy learning basic rules of play and bidding even to have heard of aggression in bridge tactics.

I asked someone else. 'They don't try enough,' he said, 'and they don't have enough stamina.'

Well, of course, thought I, part of that is true. We have never been taught to try as much as men. We have actually been taught not to care about winning, not to beat men. They may not marry us. But stamina! That was a different matter.

20

My indignation knew no bounds, although I did not show it. I was seeking information, not an argument. But I *knew* that it had been proved women had more stamina than men.

Then I asked Rixi Markus.

'Women!' she said. 'Don't talk to me about women bridge players! They are hopeless! They don't concentrate properly. They are too busy gazing around the room.' She waved her hands around. 'They're always looking here. Looking there. Not looking at the cards. Thinking about clothes, and people, and parties, instead of thinking about the cards.'

I went away very thoughtful. When people said women lacked stamina in bridge, they meant concentration. And once again, were we not brought up not to concentrate properly, not to look too earnest, too serious? Concentrating properly was part of trying too hard. Did our mothers not tell us to look pretty, smiling, attractive? Not to frown.

Perhaps, after all, the same handicaps operated in bridge as in all other areas of endeavour. Perhaps it all went back to sex-role conditioning. What appeared to be an activity of the brain, one in which women should do as well as men, where women even had some advantages, was a skill that required the same characteristics that girls from birth had been taught not to use, to hide, to pretend they did not possess. They must not be too competitive. Boys would not like it. They must not be too aggressive. It was unladylike. They must not be too ambitious or serious. They were meant to look pretty, sweet, demure. Above all, they must not try too hard. Boys did not like being beaten, and after all, were we not put on earth to please the boys and the men?

I would, I decided, write a book about women and bridge. I had already written books on sex-role conditioning, and I would further illustrate the argument by reference to how women performed at bridge. So I sat down at a typewriter in the press room at Biarritz and started the first chapter. After that I put it aside, but did not forget it. I started observing and listening.

CHAPTER 3

Bangkok and the Questionnaire

My next step was the Bourkes and Bangkok. Not long after returning to Australia from Biarritz, I decided to go to Bangkok for the Far Eastern Championships. Paul was in the Australian Open Team, so I could do some kibitzing and I knew several of the players in the women's team. Nor was the sex-role conditioning theory completely convincing. Competitive, aggressive women with plenty of brains abound at the bridge table, women with plenty of spare time. And what about the Asian women? Asian women living and playing in Australia did very well, and on visits to Japan and China I had noticed how smart and quick young Asian girls were in the shops. Surely older Asian women should be very good at bridge, and as bridge players tend to come from the moneyed class, there would be cheap labour in the house. I visualised them sitting and playing all day long.

The time had also come to stop just thinking about the subject, and do some positive research. So I went to Tim Bourke, who, with the possible exception of Keith McNeil, has the biggest bridge library in Australia. He was able to direct me to what had been written about women and bridge (not much), and then he and his wife, Margaret, an Australian international player, helped me draw up a list of questions for interviewing players. I particularly wanted to interview Asian women.

In Bangkok, I soon discovered two things. Although most

22

Asian women have plenty of time and help in the house, they are far more conditioned not to succeed and face even higher hurdles to success than Western women. Asian men, generally speaking, have a far stricter view about a woman's place being in the home and believe they should be supportive, obedient, passive, sweet, demure and dependent. No matter how wealthy Asian women are, they have even less freedom than their counterparts in America, Australia and Europe—not good material for success at bridge, or in anything.

It also became apparent that top bridge players are difficult to interview. They tend not to keep appointments, or not to be available at all. On the surface they appear to have plenty of time between matches in competitions or congresses. In practice, they want to spend that time talking hands or not talking at all, resting from bridge. It was obviously not going to be possible to interview the number of top players necessary to get a representative sample of their thoughts on this subject.

Yet it seemed important to find if there were any consistent characteristics that made up, firstly, a good bridge player, and, secondly, a good woman bridge player. Did they tend not to have children, for example? Or did they need money or a co-operative husband? If any of these attributes were essential, then it would reduce considerably the field from which top players would emerge. It could be similar to women in business or in professions. The number who reach the top are few because the number from which they can be selected dwindles rapidly. Because of motherhood, most of them, including many of the most efficient, drop out of the workforce.

When I returned from Bangkok I turned my interview questions into a questionnaire, intending to collect lists of players to whom to send it. Christmas came and went, and early in 1983, the IBPA Yearbook arrived. It included a list of members of the IBPA. What better people to consult on women and bridge? IBPA members give considerable thought to the game, observe players constantly, and regularly write about it. They are also often top players. Although it seemed somewhat presumptuous, I decided to send them the questionnaire. Surely enough would reply to give a sufficiently large sample? Sociologists agree that 35 replies makes a survey statistically valid.

Then came the next big surprise. The most marvellous replies came from all round the world, not only replies, but offers of help. Nearly 50% of IBPA members replied. This reinforced another view of mine. One day I had to make a rather shame-faced confession to my collected grown-up family. They had been trying to run me to earth for several days.

'I'm afraid you must accept the fact,' I said, 'that your mother is a nut.'

'How come, Mum?' one asked, not looking at all surprised.

'Well, I've been playing bridge every day and night for weeks and I'll be playing it for the next four weekends. And then I'll be going to a bridge congress for a week.'

'Well, you never could do things by halves,' another contributed.

This was true. When I fell in love, I fell madly and passionately in love. When I became a mother, I had to have four children. As only the best was good enough for those children, I toiled away writing my children's books to earn extra money. Every committee I joined, I did more than my fair share of work. When I discovered the women's movement I spent night and day at meetings, discussion groups, conferences, lobbying politicians and writing submissions to better conditions for women. When finally, at the age of 49, I returned to manage my father's business, in which I had started working at the age of 12, I worked 80 hours a week.

So, when I took up bridge, was it any wonder I became obsessed? I was not alone. For some time as I met more bridge players and grew to know their good and bad points, observed them at the table, and gazed around at congresses, the belief had slowly been growing that most bridge players were nuts. I guess 'obsessed' is the more polite description. The response to my questionnaire confirmed this idea. There is something very different about the bridge world. It has a community of interests and a comradeship quite different from other activities, and while being awash with egotists and people with strange behavioural quirks, there is also tremendous warmth there. I feel sure that from no other group of people would there have been such an interesting response to a similar questionnaire.

These questionnaires are printed in full in Appendix 1, and the lists of those who answered them in Appendix 2. Some who received it early may see additional questions. Some comments in early answers made it apparent that sex (as distinct from gender) had a bearing on women's achievement at bridge, and it also seemed necessary to know more about the background of men players as well as women. I did plan to send new questionnaires to those who had already returned them, but, as the final sample was so large, this was not necessary.

The main question asked was are men 'more successful at bridge than women'? The replies were as one would expect, and are set out in Table 1.

Several men qualified their replies by saying some women were as good as men, and the most frequently quoted names in this context were Rixi Markus, Helen Sobel, Dorothy Hayden Truscott, Mary Ann Farrell, and 'your own Norma Borin'.

The answers to the next question, asking for reasons, were also as had been anticipated but were not expressed in as clearcut a manner. It was interesting that the reasons given to

TABLE 1

	Men who replied	Women who replied
Men better	89.69%	84.12%
Women better	2.42%	4.61%
Men better at top level but not at club level	7.87%	11.29%

me at Biarritz by only four people, were confirmed by over 200 respondents. There were, however, many variations, many additional reasons, and many queries raised that gave much cause to ponder. Fortunately, only ten made such comments as: 'Because they win more' or 'It's obvious'. Everyone *knows* men win more at bridge, just as everyone knows there are more male politicians, lawyers, doctors, business people etc. What we want to discover is *why*.

One problem was that people said the same thing in different ways, but in the final analysis, the reasons fell into five main categories:

1. Men are more aggressive.
2. Men are more competitive and ambitious.
3. Men concentrate more and have more stamina.
4. Men have more opportunities.
5. Men are more logical and women too emotional.

There is nothing particularly new here, but we need to ask if these factors are true, and if they are, why? Why should these apply to a game of mental skill, which can be learnt and played in the home, as much, for example, as to top professional or business appointments?

A closer analysis of the five basic reasons and the more specific answers give a clear picture of why, generally speaking, women do not succeed more at bridge.

CHAPTER 4

'A War, Not a Game'

'The trouble with women,' said one male respondent, 'is that they treat bridge as a game. They do not realise it is a war.' A leading woman player agreed. 'Men see bridge as a battle,' she said, 'which they have to win.' Many other men agreed: 'women lack viciousness'; 'they only go for the jugular when their young are concerned'; 'men are better suited for the rough and tumble atmosphere'; 'women are not prepared to cut a friend's throat for an overtrick'; 'women lack the killer instinct'; 'women are not tough enough'; 'men are taught to be more aggressive from birth'.

Many replies from women players were similar: 'Men are taught to be aggressive'; 'men have a macho superiority complex'; 'women are timid, while men use calculated aggression'; 'women don't bid or lead aggressively enough'; 'men are more daring'; 'men use physical aggression at the table'.

These few quotes give a taste of how the people replying to the questionnaires saw the difference between men and women players. By far the main reasons given for women not being more successful were that they were not aggressive or not competitive enough. Table 2 summarizes this.

These reasons were given in different ways. Some said it more colourfully, but mostly the replies were simply 'not aggressive enough', 'men are taught to be aggressive from birth', 'women not competitive enough', 'men more competitive', or 'men more ambitious'. It was tempting to combine

TABLE 2

	Men who replied	Women who replied
Women are not aggressive enough	36.36%	22.22%
Women are not competitive enough	54.54%	66.66%

these replies, and in some contexts they are the same. 'To lack aggression in bidding', for example, is the same as 'not being competitive enough in bidding'. However, in most contexts they are different, and I decided to treat them separately, for three reasons.

Firstly, there is a difference between aggressive and competitive behaviour at the bridge table. Some players, usually men, exude an aggression that goes far beyond competitiveness in bidding or play. They bully and berate their female partners; they flip each card down in a sharp, aggressive manner; and sometimes they demonstrate aggression by ignoring a woman partner and opponent and joking with a male opponent, sometimes at the expense of one of the women. These things can be very intimidating for some women and result in bad play or lack of confidence. Admittedly, there are some women who also behave in this manner, abusing their male partner, usually a husband, but when this happens the woman tends to be talked about. It is 'unseemly', 'not like a woman at all'. Most women playing with men inferior to them accept their mistakes patiently. The worst verbal abusers are nearly always men against women, and it must affect the women's game.

Secondly, several of the replies that said 'not competitive enough' were definitely not referring to aggression. They qualified it by saying women did not try enough, did not work hard enough, or were not ambitious enough. People can be fiercely competitive at the table, at a game, at anything in life,

28

without being aggressive. They can be determined, hard working. 'Obsessive' was the word many applied to men players.

Thirdly, many people used both terms about the difference between men and women players, so they obviously believed there was a difference. Also, far more used the word competitive than the word aggressive. In fact, the number of references to women's lack of competitiveness was the most informative and significant factor to emerge from the replies. It was described in various ways by both men and women. Women were said to be not as competitive as men, not as ambitious, not prepared to work as hard at bridge, not willing to practise enough, to discuss hands, to read enough bridge books, were more interested in the social side of bridge, more concerned about social chat, coffee, talking about clothes, parties, children. Here are some comments from men.

'Thank goodness, women are primarily feminine and secondly competitive. Men can be competitive to the exclusion of all else'; 'men play serious bridge'; 'few ladies invest the time, money and brains necessary'; 'the male pictures himself as a winner'; 'men make bridge an enormous part of their life'; 'men have more will to win'; 'women play bridge as a part-time activity'; 'women do not expect to win'; 'the drive to win is much stronger in men'; 'man sees his very life on the line'; 'women treat bridge as a recreation, hobby, a diversion'; 'women do not take games seriously'; 'women treat bridge as a game; men know it is not'; 'women's bridge is too social'; 'women are too lazy and not prepared to do their homework'. So one could go on. Many of the women agreed: 'Men are encouraged to succeed'; 'men are more competitive by nature'; 'men are more single-minded'; 'women can't compete'; 'women do not have the will to win'; 'women are not so interested in winning'; 'men are more dedicated' are just a few of the remarks women made.

Many men qualified their critical remarks. 'Women are

29

more cautious, more conservative and safety-conscious, what I call the "baby-syndrome" brought about by their mothering role'; 'women care more about people'; 'women are more concerned to please men than to win'; 'women concentrate on important things, such as raising a family. This may change'; 'women quite sensibly have other interests: sex, marriage, home'; 'women have to be more well-rounded in order to manage a household'; 'women spend less time on bridge, men have no commonsense'; 'men tend to take anything seriously whereas women tend to consider the practical value of things.' Perhaps this Asian comment best summed up men's attitudes: 'If women devoted as much time to bridge as men, the basic unit of society, the family, would be adversely affected, and we would have a generation of children brought up without maternal care . . . it is not that women are inferior. . . .'

These comments were undoubtedly meant to be complimentary to show that they appreciated that women were not succeeding at bridge because they were fulfilling a much more important role, rearing a family. In fact, this male attitude of flattering women about their family role is one of the many ways men keep them in that role. Men do not honestly believe bridge is less important or fulfilling than child-rearing. If they did, they would spend less time on it. They are happy to continue being highly successful at bridge, or other activities, while women stay at home and carry out the often frustrating and low-status role of housewife. It is the men who decide the different roles. This has been dealt with much more fully in a later chapter.

Women respondents agreed wholeheartedly with the male views that women had less time for bridge: 'Women tend to diversify'; 'women have a double job and other priorities'; 'I like to spend more time with my children'; 'women cannot give as much time as men because they want to give themselves to their children, to *living*'; 'women want more

30

time for their family'; 'women want to spend time on other things, their work, music, reading, etc'; 'men have fewer responsibilities and distractions'; 'women are child-bearing and -rearing during the important years'; 'men who choose bridge can give all their time to it, women with children feel a first obligation to those children and the home'; 'women consider home duties more important'; etc.

Whatever the reasons, the overwhelming response was that women do not try enough, care enough or work hard enough at competitive sports or games. Nor is this surprising. There is statistical proof that men prefer, as wives, women less clever than they are. Toys, children's stories, advertisements, the attitudes of schools, the church, peers and relatives all influence girls to be passive, supportive, emotional, unselfish and to grow up to be wives and mothers. In the same way boys are taught to be aggressive, competitive, tough, strong, ambitious, and to grow up to be doctors, lawyers, electricians, plumbers, accountants, captains of industry.

There is no need to produce proof here of this sex-role conditioning. It was observed and noted by a number of men replying. To quote just a few, David Askew of Australia wrote that 'there is no wonder women do not often reach the top in what is a fiercely competitive game . . . women are taught to be acquiescent . . . these characteristics are induced as early as the cradle and reinforced by sexual stereotypes in society and at school.' 'Men are brought up to be ambitious,' said A. Boekhorst of the Netherlands, 'and women to focus on other things.' 'Women are taught not to be competitive,' said Svend Novrup of Denmark, while Ib Lundby of Denmark said 'women are educated to take the responsibility for home and children'. Cariolan Neamtzu of Romania commented on women's 'different education', while Michael Becker of the US said 'women are not encouraged by society to use their intelligence in business or mental sports'. Max Rebattu of the Netherlands said 'it is hard for women to concentrate on one thing, because of their socialised background. But this may change in the future.'

'Women know men do not like to lose,' said Robert Bonomi of the US, 'so they act to avoid that'. 'Females are socialised not to be aggressive,' said David Watkins of Australia, 'and they are more co-operative and pleasant'. 'Women are less suited by training,' said James Jacoby of the US, 'for a competitive and intelligent game'. 'Women have not been brought up to challenge so keenly,' said David Brown of England, and from Alfred Sheinwold came the wise remark 'women do not neglect their children and family to play in a tournament. It would be better if men were less fanatical and neglectful. They should be equalised down rather than women moving towards male attitudes.'

Other men and several women made similar remarks. Another interesting fact was the number of replies which compared bridge to golf and tennis. Many made such comments as 'women are not as good at bridge, just as they are not as good at tennis or golf'. The analogy is false because golf and tennis are physical sports and bridge is a mental pastime, but it is true that women do not succeed as well at these two sports as they should, mainly because they do not try hard enough. What is significant is that there are certain sports at which girls are outstandingly successful, for example swimming and gymnastics. It is tempting to speculate that girls succeed here because they can train and try enormously hard without appearing too determined. When they compete in swimming we do not see the pain experienced while swimming, only the smiling young faces popping up at the end. Nor do we see the hours of pain and stress the gymnasts endure, only the beauty and grace of the final result.

Tennis is quite different. The effort, concentration and aggression of players is clearly visible, and is not met with approval in females. For years Chris Evert has been called 'the ice maiden' (she is merely concentrating), Billie-Jean King was labelled over-aggressive (she was merely fighting), and Martina Navratilova is regularly described as a computer. Evonne Goolagong, on the other hand, was 'everybody's darling', and Pam Shriver plays with a perpetual smile on her face. But we all know who wins the most. Women players not only have to contend with their opponents but with attitudes as to how women should behave and look. No one criticises McEnroe, Connors, or Lendl for their intense concentration and training. The reason a few leading women stay so far ahead of the others is because not many are mentally strong enough to stand up against the criticism society places on too aggressive women.

Women are subject to so many pressures other than merely winning. Is it any wonder they are not aggressive or competitive enough or do not try hard enough at the bridge table? It is not that they are inferior, but simply because they are taught it is unfeminine to try.

CHAPTER 5

The Story of the Naked Lady

To make a point effectively, people often repeat a good story about different people. This makes it colourful, if not necessarily true. Perhaps the story of the naked lady fits this category.

In *Omar Sharif's Life in Bridge*[2] he claims that as a test of his concentration his friends sat a beautiful young naked woman next to his partner at the table, and he did not notice her. Two of my correspondents told me the same story about Terence Reese. I find it hard to believe that even in the eccentric bridge world, all these naked ladies were paraded around these bridge rooms, unless, of course, it was in all-male clubs where possibly a situation exists similar to those bucks' parties where young naked women regularly leap out of cakes? Anyway, whether the story is true or not is irrelevant. It is a good one and it demonstrates the extent of men's concentration when playing bridge. This, we are told, is in great contrast to women.

Lack of concentration or stamina was the third most common reason given in the questionnaires for women's lack of success, as shown in Table 3.

Added together here are the replies that said 'lack of stamina' to those that said 'lack of concentration'. To say women lacked stamina was an error in word usage. There is statistical evidence to show that women, although not as strong, have more stamina than men.[3] But, alas, there is also

TABLE 3

	Men who replied	Women who replied
Women do not concentrate	30.30%	41.26%

evidence that women's concentration does fail in bridge. An example was sent to me of the French men's and women's trials that were held at the same time over nine days. The women's results were as good as the men's 'for three or four days, *but* as the play went on (64 boards a day, a total of 448 boards) the women's results fell away badly'. 'Women tire in long events' or 'women are fine for a two-session event but I prefer a man partner for anything longer' were typical of other male remarks. Top women players agreed. Typical are 'women don't concentrate. Except my partner. She plays like a man'; 'women lack concentration. Even top players go to pieces over a long session'; 'women are learning to concentrate. They have not tried hard enough in the past'; 'women instead of playing bridge are worrying about their dress, catching a husband. But it is changing now. Young women today do not care what they look like.'

There are many reasons for women's lack of concentration, and they are mainly concerned with children. Firstly, as indicated by several of the quotes from men in the last chapter, a woman's main concern is her children. To sum this up Colonel Sharma of India said 'a woman is not able to give the single-minded devotion and mental concentration necessary, due to varied interests and commitments to family.' The women agree wholeheartedly. Dorothy Hayden Truscott said, 'women always have part of their minds on their children. If men are playing at home, the children could let the water flow right through the ceiling, or the dinner could be burnt to a crisp in the oven, and the men would not notice. But,' she added 'what an asinine way to run your life.'

Asinine it may be, but it is the way to win. Apart from their minds being divided between children and bridge, one frequently sees top women bridge players dashing from home where they have cooked the meal or put the children to bed to the bridge table. Men seldom do this. They can usually walk out of the house with a clear, undistracted mind, and leave these jobs to their wife.

Secondly, because it is assumed that children are mainly the woman's responsibility, she feels far more guilty than a man if something goes wrong at home. So she worries about them more. One leading player said 'whenever I am called to the telephone I think "something's gone wrong with the children!" It is hard to take my mind off them completely.' How can women concentrate fully under this pressure?

Thirdly, it goes even deeper. By bringing up children, many women actually lose their ability to concentrate. This does not mean a woman's brain is altered by child-bearing, as some maintain. There is no proof of this. It is the daily and constant contact with small children that fragments a woman's concentration. Whatever she starts doing is immediately interrupted. She cannot even conduct an unbroken conversation on the telephone. Whatever she does is immediately undone. She spends countless hours talking to and listening to children, and no matter how much she loves them, no matter how endearing they may be at times, this continuous contact lacks mental stimulation, a sharing of interests, anything really to occupy the mind. It is impossible for a young mother even to think coherently of intelligent things, because her thoughts are constantly interrupted. Instead of coherent thought, there is frustration, irritation, fragmentation. This is demonstrated in Ann Oakley's *Housewife*[4], a sociological study of housework.

'Women have so many idle moments,' said one woman player, 'that she becomes used to noticing other things. She will sit down at the bridge table and notice another woman's

36

ring. A man is completely unaware of it. He is totally absorbed in the game.' 'Because men have mental stimulation at work,' said another young woman, 'their minds remain more disciplined.'

Fourthly, a woman's concentration tends to lapse because when things get difficult she is able to take the easy way out. Part of the upbringing that has taught her not to compete, not to be too clever, also offers her the 'soft option' of giving in. If it is 'unfeminine' for her to win, then why not be feminine and make excuses, why put in that extra competitive effort that is supposed to be against her real nature?

Note how often, when the going gets tough at the bridge table, and mistakes start being made, a woman 'feels tired' or 'has a headache'. Men seldom act like this. The effort to concentrate becomes greater as a tournament progresses and the day gets late. Towards the end of any competitive game or sport is when players need to dig their heels in, hang on, try even harder, keep up their concentration no matter how hard the struggle. It is very easy at this all-important stage to decide 'it does not really matter', 'I don't care that much', 'winning is not important'. Note how often women will ask 'how many hands to go?' or when things go wrong say, 'it doesn't really matter' or 'it is just a game, after all'.

And women have every excuse to give up in these final stages. That is how they see life. It is seldom that little girls, like little boys, have been lectured on 'how important it is to succeed', 'how one must win at all costs', 'how one must strive to get on in life', 'how one must be strong and tough'. Little girls are taught they will achieve their aims by smiling sweetly, being a little weak, a little incompetent. It gives them an entirely false idea of life, of course, because mothers have to be very tough, always enduring, ever strong and endlessly patient. Few see the contradiction in this, for it is only in the role that is seen as strictly female, motherhood, where these attributes are acceptable in women. They do not apply to a game as useless as bridge. Two very strong-minded competitive women bridge players supported these views. Rixi Markus said, 'one of my boyfriends said to me "I love you but I love my work more". But a woman is expected to put her emotions first, so if she fails in a game, no one blames her.' Kathy Boardman of New Zealand said 'it is considered feminine to wilt'.

Fifthly, women's concentration suffers through male attitudes. Although there are plenty of myths about women keeping men waiting, the reality is that once the courting days are over (if they exist any longer) women spend an enormous amount of time waiting for men, waiting on men, listening to men. This is part of their supportive, caring, less important role in life. They wait for them to come home from work, they wait for them to decide where or when holidays are to be spent, they mostly wait while men play sport or games. Study top bridge competition. How often do you see girlfriends or wives patiently sitting beside a male player, hours on end? How seldom do you see a man kibitzing a woman player? No matter how close they are to a woman, they will not give up the time to watch.

Also, study the style of leading bridge players. Most top men will spend what often seems endless time thinking about their bidding, their leading, their discards, their play. Some players think too long and quite unnecessarily, but there is no doubt that, given more consideration, difficult bridge problems can often be solved. Women seldom think long enough at bridge. They are not expected to. They are not allowed to. Men have never waited on women's words or thoughts. If a woman does think for any length of time, men at the table become impatient. Paul Lavings often tells me I should think longer, but when I do, he becomes impatient. If I point this out, he is either apologetic or says, 'but there was no need to think there. It was quite obvious.' Maybe it was obvious to him, but it wasn't to me. So even when women try

38

to think longer and concentrate more on a particular problem, their line of thought is often broken by men's irritation.

There are other ways men break women's concentration. They tease women, joke with them, chat them up. The best women players are not affected by this, but lesser players can be. In the trials for the Australian Women's Teams for Seattle held in Canberra in 1984, in the last match of the day, my team was playing against the team running second. Firstly, we were interrupted by a child, and then several men came and started discussing the cricket scores with our opponents. Imagine two or three women walking up to a men's team playing off for the Olympic team and joking about the cricket scores!

Whatever the various reasons, there can be little doubt that a woman's ability to concentrate at the bridge table is inferior to a man's.

CHAPTER 6

No 'Equal Rights to Leisure Time'

'Women,' wrote Jakob Armannson of Iceland 'do not have equal rights to leisure time'. 'Babies,' wrote Fritz Babsch of Austria, 'stop many promising careers'.

The above two aspects of being female—motherhood and different expectations about how women should spend their time—were mentioned in many of the questionnaires. It has already been shown that they result in the woman bridge-player's lack of aggression, competitiveness, willingness to work hard, and concentration. It must now be taken further. As already said, many of the men qualified their harsh criticisms of women's bridge by saying family responsibilities were important for women and women did not have the same opportunities.

As also already pointed out, the women respondents agreed wholeheartedly. Almost universally they said how difficult it was to run a home, work outside the home, give time to their children and friends, and work at bridge. 'And if I did not keep up my job,' said more than one, 'I could not afford to play bridge'. Indeed, the fact that a lower proportion of women who received questionnaires returned them, may be yet another indication that women bridge players have less time than men to give to matters not essential.

Table 4 summarizes the replies.

TABLE 4: WOMEN HAVE LESS OPPORTUNITIES

	Men who replied	Women who replied
Because of family responsibility	24.84%	65.07%
Lack of money	3.63%	11.11%
Men start younger and keep playing	4.84%	7.93%
Women don't play enough rubber bridge	2.42%	6.34%
Women don't play enough professional bridge	2.42%	4.76%
Men's attitudes prevent women being in good teams and partnerships	—	23.80%

Although most of the above referred to the handicap women suffered through family responsibilities, there were a significant number of other reasons given to warrant discussion. Many of these were the *result* of motherhood, when a woman gives up her independence, her money-making ability and her right to choose her lifestyle. Others, however, stem from *attitudes* to how women—particularly young women—should behave. Let us look at these first. They are more interesting and less recognised.

Firstly, a significant number of replies pointed out that very few young women play bridge during the early formative years which are necessary to develop high bridge skills. Examine any bridge club and see the groups of young men who sit round during the weekend or late at night, playing bridge or talking about it. A young girl would seldom be allowed to do that. Her parents and relatives would tell her it was bad for her health, her social life, her education. Further, young women are not expected to have idle moments. 'If you have time for that,' someone would say,

41

'come and help with the dishes'. Or looking after siblings. Or getting herself a job, a boyfriend or a new dress. Even if they were motivated to join the young men players, they would tend to be cold-shouldered by these all-male groups. It was quite clear in a number of the questionnaires that many men considered women 'a good thing' for the lighter side of bridge, to make tea, 'as dancing partners', as bed partners.

A number of people used women's complete lack of success in the top echelons of chess as proof that women's brains are different from men's. There is absolutely no evidence of this, only plenty of theories.[5] But just as no young woman would be allowed to 'waste' her weekends at the local bridge club, even less would she be allowed the time to become a good chess player. No one would ever leave a young woman or girl uninterrupted long enough to play even one long game of chess, let alone several. No one would say about her, 'don't interrupt her—not even for meals. Leave her be. She's so clever', in the way they talk about young boy prodigies.

Take a superwoman like Dorothy Hayden Truscott, with her extraordinary list of successes, and any woman at the top of her profession has to be a superwoman. She could fit in playing rubber bridge, playing competition bridge, teaching bridge, with running a household and caring for many children. She could dash here and there, quickly and frequently, from home to bridge. She could never do that with chess, which requires such protracted and uninterrupted thinking time. Nor would the financial rewards be there. Most women who play top bridge need to earn money as well as everything else. This is hard with chess. The impossibility of a busy housewife playing serious championship chess makes comparison impossible with the problems with top bridge.

The wife of one of Australia's leading bridge administrators gives a further example of how young women are not expected to play bridge. She tells the marvellous story of going, as a young girl, to the local bridge club. Being

42

inexperienced in bridge ways, and it being a hot night, she wore a pretty, short, white lace frock. 'I'm afraid you've come to the wrong place,' said one of the older woman players. 'The disco is next door.' It was obviously considered unlikely that a young woman would want to play bridge.

So most women are deprived, in building their bridge careers, of playing in the most formative learning years.

The second way women's bridge is influenced by attitudes concerns husbands. How the 63 women who answered the questionnaire described their marital status is set out in Tables 5, 6 and 7.

TABLE 5

	Women who replied
Married	74.60%
Divorced	15.87%
Widowed	4.76%
Never married	4.76%
Children	77.77%
No children	17.46%

In regard to husband's attitudes the returns showed the following:

TABLE 6

	Women who replied
Husbands play a lot	76.19%
Husbands play very little or not at all	15.87%
Never married	4.76%
No answer	3.17%

TABLE 7

	Women who replied
Husbands very supportive	17.60%
Not supportive and now divorced	6.34%
A little supportive	11.11%
Never married	4.76%
No answer	3.17%

Of those still married every single one said their husbands were either most or a little co-operative about their bridge. One said, 'he wants me to play more than I do', and a significant number indicated that they became bridge players because their boyfriends or husbands were committed players.

So what of all those women who may have wanted to play bridge (like myself), but never could because their husbands did not play, or who played, but because of family commitments, could not play seriously. Until I became a feminist my life revolved around the men in my life. From the age of 12 until I was married I did what my father wanted, worked in his business, and played a little bridge. Then I took up my husband's interests, rowing, ski-ing, entertaining mostly his friends. I took up bridge seriously only after our marriage broke down—it was not the cause of it. Even though I had the time, with my children grown-up, I could never have devoted the time to bridge, I do now. It would have been tolerated whenever my husband was away or out, but I was always expected to be home the weekends he was. I could have argued for my rights, as I did in regard to travelling for my job, but the resultant tension over something like bridge would have made it not worthwhile.

More than anything else, what of those women (goodness knows how many) with top bridge brains, who never played bridge at all, because they followed their husbands' interests? This fact of life dramatically reduces the number of top women bridge players, and is completely analogous with every other field of female endeavour. At every stage of a business, professional or artistic career, very able women drop out either because of families or lack of their husband's co-operation, or because they have to move to follow their husband's career. It helps a man if his wife is a co-operative supporter of his bridge or any other activity. If, however, a wife is against it, a man, because he is financially independent and allowed by community attitudes to follow his own interests, can not only play, but give a large part of his time to the game. Many women, because their husbands are obsessed players, take up the game seriously themselves. They are not always the most able players.

The third main area in which attitudes handicap women players is in their selection of partners. As everyone knows, a good partner or the best partner for any particular player, is essential for obtaining top results. Observation, discussion and the answers to the questionnaire would seem to indicate that women are frequently disadvantaged in this aim. This is discussed in full in the next chapter.

Having dealt with the way attitudes deprive women of equal opportunities in bridge, let us just briefly look at the other areas. There were several other reasons that a few respondents gave for women's lack of success. One was that they do not play as much rubber bridge for money as men (when one's life is, so-to-speak, at stake). Another was that they cannot travel enough. A third that they do not compete full-time in a game that is becoming increasingly professional. A woman's handicap in these three areas is because she is mostly married, a mother and dependent. She does not have the money, the time or the freedom.

In regard to women having money it is interesting to note that very few of the female respondents perceived themselves

45

as disadvantaged, as shown in Table 8, when asked if they had any money problems.

TABLE 8

	Women who replied
No money problems	82.53%
Have money problems	11.11%
No view	6.30%

Many of those who said they had no money problems did qualify the statement by remarks such as 'not really', 'not on the whole', 'I would like to travel more', or 'I live within my budget'. The fact that generally speaking these leading players did not perceive themselves to have money problems in this expensive pastime indicates that lack of money must keep large numbers of capable dependent women away.

On the same theme another interesting result was the paucity or lack of help in the house enjoyed by most women players. This is shown in Table 9.

TABLE 9

	Women who replied
Some help in the house	50.79%
No help in the house	41.53%
No answer	6.30%

Most of those who did have help in the house, said it was mostly only one day or half a day a week. Only the Asian women had considerable help. The figures amazed me. It surely was a final proof of how much the women bridge players had to do, and also that although they may not have

46

money problems, they certainly do not have access to the money to give themselves the independence, time and freedom necessary to give a full commitment to the game.

CHAPTER 7

'A Man if I Want to Win,
but Socially I Prefer a Woman'

Some men may believe the above statement is a compliment to women. In fact, it is one more proof that men see women as suitable for those areas in living that bring the smaller rewards and the lower status. Let us look back at Table 4, setting out the reasons women have less opportunities to succeed in bridge. It is interesting to note that 24% of women respondents gave male attitudes to partnerships as one factor discriminating against them. Not one man gave this as a reason, although two did maintain that male attitudes deprived women of the chance to compete in open teams.

When one looks at the men's replies about partners as set out in Table 10, it is clear the leading men feel strongly that even good women players do not make the best partners, yet they do not perceive that this attitude discriminates against women's progress. They rationalise their views by saying 'women are not as good'. Further, when they do play with them, they often alter their style of game. When the partnership or team with a woman in it then does not succeed they often blame the woman. Again, a microcosm of what happens in life in general.

Another interesting fact that emerged was that although the top players around the world almost universally preferred men partners (because they were better, or tougher, or more logical, or more competitive), some of them chose men at the top of their careers, but later changed to women because they

TABLE 10

	Men who replied
Preferred a man partner	55.75%
Preferred a woman partner	22.42%
Chose according to ability, not gender	20.60%
No view	1.21%

were more pleasant, amiable, co-operative or understanding. Some of them also made remarks such as 'if I play for fun I prefer women', or 'a man if I want to win, but socially I prefer a woman'. One even said 'of course if a woman was young, attractive etc, I would make an exception'; and another 'it depends on which girl'; and yet another 'a woman would have to be good, pretty and pleasant'.

A number of the players who preferred a woman said they always played with their wives, and others gave the same reasons as above of amiability (shades of Jane Austen), with such comments as 'women do not strive for perfection, so are not so rude, they accept error'; 'for friendly bridge I prefer a woman'; 'I prefer facing something pretty, kinder, willing to improve, more flexible and understanding'; 'women take the game less seriously and are more pleasant to play with'; 'women are more pleasant'; 'a nice girl is better than a man'; 'now I am older and can appreciate the finer things in life, I prefer a woman'; 'women are more co-operative and therefore often more successful'; 'I play bridge as a game'; 'I find men more egotistical and that personality conflicts are much more comfortable with a woman'. The problem women face in finding a good male partner (the terrible conflict women face generally in getting to the top in any area) is surely summed up in this classic male (even if probably tongue-in-cheek) answer: 'I do not like to have as a partner a woman who is, intellectually, my equal or superior. Moreover, I do not like to have a fool as a partner. Then again, if she is ugly I may not like to play with her, while too attractive a partner may upset my concentration. So, I could play only with a woman who is intelligent, but not really my equal, and neither too beautiful nor ugly. Is it not asking too much?'

What emerges from these comments is that although women may not be generally considered as good as men at bridge, many men find them more pleasant and more amiable, a fact which conflicts strangely with the attitude of other men indicated later on the subject of men as non-playing captains of women's teams, 'keeping the girls apart'. What also does emerge is that generally the men stick together. Pat Sheinwold in her amusing *Husbands and Other Men I've Played With*[6] tells how her husband had a regular rubber bridge male four at their home. As Pat worked on her bridge and improved, she 'was certain the boys would ask her into their game'. Such was not to be, until the inevitable night they lost their fourth (what a familiar happening!) and asked her to play. It went very well for some time and she felt it would be permanent, but 'in time the men replaced their fourth, forgot about me, so I went back to playing duplicate'.

A significant number of men respondents also said they would find it hard to spend a lot of time discussing bridge with women or going away with them to congresses because their wives would be jealous. And to be honest, when a man or woman play and travel together regularly, other players do tend to think they sleep together. So it can be said that there are many obstacles to a top woman player acquiring a top man player as a partner. This must affect their results.

Nor can one always blame the men. Although there are many women who would make good partners, other women have irritating habits which give a bad impression of their sex. They talk when the director is giving instructions, they

50

laugh too loudly, they leave lipstick on coffee cups, and put make-up on at the table. One of my close friends tells a story against me. One day she said to me, 'I don't know why you're always standing up for women. They drive me mad at the table'.

'I know,' I said, 'some of them drive me mad, too. But it's all the fault of men'. She gave me a despairing, 'you-are-hopeless' glare. But it is true. All these irritating habits have been acquired, when young, to please men. Women are expected to keep conversation going, so often their talk is pointless. They laugh loudly to attract attention, they are taught from an early age to put on make-up to please men. Dorothy Hayden Truscott, discussing the fact that women talk at the table, said, 'I always say that women invented good manners'.

Another factor that causes men to downgrade women's bridge is that with a mixed partnership, the man tends to think he is better, takes control, does not trust his partner in regard to leading and bidding, and thus often plays bad bridge. Then, when failure results, he blames her. I made a resolution that this would be a bridge book without a single hand. In typical female fashion, I do not read nearly enough bridge books, because I get bored with hands. But in the context of this book, this bidding sequence at least demands to be published. It came with a questionnaire returned by a European player, typed by his wife, and accompanied by a note from her that said, 'he is not nearly as bad as he sounds, but I have had to give up playing with him. Here is one of our last hands together. I opened with 1◇. He responded 1NT. The bidding continued: 2◇; 2NT; 3◇; 3NT; 4◇; 4NT. DOUBLE. Down three, vulnerable. Everyone else was in 2◇, making four. His gosh was not exactly amusing.'

There are constant references to and jokes about this well-known mixed pairs no-trump syndrome, where the men bid no-trumps so they will get to play the hand. It certainly militates against the best results. Pat Sheinwold gives many examples of men dominating the play. After a male opponent, playing with his wife, opened no-trumps with a 5-card major (not in their system), she found herself wondering if no-trumps and 'I'm head of the house' were synonymous. 'I pay all the bills so I'll play all the no-trumps'.[7] And again, when the men decided to play against the women, she again thought perhaps the bidding would go, '1 no-trump; 2 no-trumps; 3 no-trumps; 4 no-trumps; 5 no-trumps; 6 no-trumps; 7 no-trumps; 8 no-trumps?'[8] Of course, it did not go like that at all, because men respect their male partners, and bid more sensibly. Pat Sheinwold, however, does share my criticism of many women players, who blame their male partners, bad luck, or 'feeling off' for bad results, instead of their own lack of hard work and application, and their unwillingness to take criticism.

When men and women do make permanent, good partnerships, they are usually very good, because of the caring and co-operative nature found in women, often lacking in men. The woman in these partnerships generally adapts to the man, learns his system, and the man is the controlling player. This does not mean that men cannot make caring partnerships with other men. Any great partnership, male or female, demands understanding and consideration for each other. I can remember when Lew Stansby and Chip Martel won the open pairs in Biarritz reading in the daily bulletin that Stansby had not told Martel he had slept badly the night before, as he did not want to worry him.

It is interesting to speculate on why the great male-female partnerships of the past no longer exist around the world bridge scene. Everyone knows the enormously important part Josephine Culbertson played in establishing the popularity of bridge in the early 1930s, not only as Ely's partner, but in her own right. Her good looks were a part of the showbiz manner in which Ely promoted bridge, as was also his deliberate introduction of sex appeal into the game, with the use of phrases such as 'squeezes', 'forcing bid', 'approach bid'. 'I have sold bridge through sex,' he wrote. 'The game brought men and women together.'[9] However, Josephine also played a very good game, and her contribution was followed by other famous mixed pair successes. Among these were the Helen Sobel-Charles Goren partnership with a most impressive list of successes in open national and international events, and Dorothy Hayden Truscott, also with an extraordinary list of successes in open bridge, playing with many partners, but particularly with B. Jay Becker. It is often said that women do not have the types of minds for original, inventive thinking, but to Dorothy Truscott is attributed the Splinter and Dopi conventions,[10] and 'to Dorothy Sims belongs the honour, which no one will wish to dispute, of being the mother of the psychic bid.'[11]

Then there is the well-known story of the young woman, written into all bridge histories, who was watching Harold S. Vanderbilt play bridge on that history-making cruise late in 1925 when they were experimenting with a new scoring system, a system that was to transform Auction Bridge to Contract Bridge. It was she who suggested 'vulnerable'. One should be thankful that her contribution was remembered, but had she been a man would her name also have been remembered? History tends to make women invisible. Had she been a man indeed she would probably have been playing rather than watching.

Why then does one no longer see these famous and productive mixed partnerships? One can only speculate. As bridge became more professional, more deadly earnest, more a war and less a game, more a means of earning a living, it is possible that men, who run this world, subconsciously decided it was time for women to be banished from the top echelons. Feminists are regularly accused of lacking a sense of humour (one has to have a good sense of humour to combat the anti-feminist jibes that are constantly made), and of keeping on about the subject. 'Things are different now,' they are told. 'You have won your battle'.

Such is not the case. There are proofs on all sides that in the academic world, as one example (and bridge belongs there) the status and promotion rate of women is declining. From Oxford in England comes the report that since the male colleges have accepted female students, not only have female results slipped, but 'the proportion of female dons (which used to be between 15–20 per cent, the highest proportion in any British university) has dropped to 7 per cent'.[12] This is reflected in Australian universities. Another recent report on the state of education in Victoria, a state of Australia, reveals that 'the number and proportion of women in higher-ranking jobs in the Education Department has declined over the past 12 years—despite equal employment policy since 1972. A department study released yesterday shows that the distribution of women teaching in Victoria is no better in 1984 than it was in 1925'.[13] A computing specialist, Susan Moont from Ontario, Canada, said in a research paper recently, 'women dislike shoot-'em-up games and lack aggressive tendencies and are thus marked for failure in the information age'.[14]

Whatever the reasons, women are no longer featuring in top male-female partnerships in bridge. Men can find perfectly good reasons, as already set out. In good faith, they believe men are better players, and because they believe this, they act according to this belief. They always play with men or they believe that when they play with women their results are not as good, and women consequently become less good. 'It is a self-perpetuating cycle,' said one of my more aware male respondents. Until female pairs or teams can win regularly at the top level, it will be hard to persuade men to change their views. And because even the top male pairs or teams find it hard to win regularly, it is going to be a long, hard struggle for the women.

Apart from the top men preferring to play with other top men, a top woman often faces problems obtaining a female player as good as she is. This does not apply so much in the US, where so many people play, but in some other countries the female ranks get rather thin at the top, and many promising partnerships are broken through pregnancy, an unco-operative husband, family illness or financial problems. One European woman player saying how hard it was to get a suitable partner, enumerated three choices—each one a problem. To play with one's husband was notoriously difficult; to play with another man put a strain on both marriages; but in settling to play with another woman, it was hard to find one who wanted to work as hard at the game and lived nearby.

On many levels attitudes prevent women obtaining partners to help them achieve their full potential.

CHAPTER 8

'Most Women are so Remarkably Illogical'

Thus wrote one leading, well-known bridge writer. Very emotive indeed, is the use of that word 'remarkably', but interesting in continuing a study of attitudes commonly held towards women and how these attitudes affect them. It may be remembered that respondents to the questionnaire listed five main reasons for women being less successful at bridge than men: lack of aggression, competitiveness, concentration, opportunities and logic. The first four are demonstrably true and I have attempted to show that what happens at the bridge table is similar to how women perform in every area of endeavour. Further, that this behavioural pattern is attributable to their upbringing (sex-role conditioning) and/or to the fact that mostly they marry and have children.

With the fifth point, however, there is reason and proof to disagree. Labelling women as 'illogical' and/or 'emotional' is one of the classic ways the establishment (men) keep women in a lower position, feeling inferior, and out of the top ranks of the work force. Let us discuss the word emotional first, as it is the easiest.

There is no doubt women burst into tears more easily than men. I have been reduced to tears several times at the bridge table, as has Pat Sheinwold and many other women. That does not prove women are more emotional. Tears are merely one of the ways that women are allowed to express their emotions, ways that show females are weak. To burst into tears is a baby response. To giggle is a trivialising response. To cover your face because embarrassed is a cowardly response. It is acceptable for women to do these. Men on the other hand are allowed actions that show their strength and that their strength is being thwarted. At the bridge table, instead of bursting into tears, they express their emotions by anger, bullying, shaking, shouting, going white, throwing their cards on the table, groaning, sighing, sarcastic words.

There is no doubt women's bridge suffers under stress more than does men's. As has already been said, girls are brought up not to win, to take the soft option when competition gets tough, to give in. But this is different from being emotional.

To turn to logic, one faces a much more complex problem. A logical or an illogical mind is hard to prove. It is tested in school and university examinations, and women do equally well in these. In day-to-day life, however, it is a matter of opinion. The reality is surely that some *people* are illogical, male or female, and some are very logical. Many women with logical minds have experienced the utter frustration of arguing with an illogical man who has more power (because he is the husband with the money, or the boss at work). Honest, intelligent logical men will admit to the same frustration in arguing with an illogical man with more power.

The difficulty of proving logic or lack of logic is revealed by the contradictory nature of the replies on this subject. It is a matter of opinion, and attitudes are not consistent. There are many different views given about women's logic, their aptitude, their abilities, as shown in Table 11. The variation in men's replies even reveals some lack of logic in some men's minds.

To begin with, there is absolutely no proof that a female brain is different from or inferior to that of a man.[5] Girls at school and university who do mathematics and sciences prove they can do at least as well as men and win top places.

TABLE 11

	Men who replied	Women who replied
There is *no* difference between the brains of men and women	12.72%	6.34%
Men are more logical	13.93%	7.93%
Men are more mathematical	7.87%	11.11%
Women are too emotional	18.78%	9.52%
Women are not disciplined enough	3.63%	—
Women are too disciplined	3.03%	—
Men are too disciplined	—	1.58%
Women do not have enough flair	3.63%	—
Women have more flair and better judgment	3.63%	—
Women lack confidence or have low self-esteem	4.24%	11.11%

There does appear to be a type of brain that excels at games like bridge and chess. In the questionnaires easily the most consistent trait was that nearly every top bridge player had a university degree, and there was an emphasis on computer people, mathematicians, scientists, economists, with a sprinkling of lawyers and doctors. This is not surprising, and does not mean much, except that a university degree usually guarantees a disciplined brain. But some people do seem able to remember hands, cards, count, etc. much more easily than others. This ability improves with practice and experience, but some people have a far greater basic ability. Because of judgment, concentration and character, these people do not always do as well in competitions, but the brain is there. In *The Walk of the Oysters*[15] Rex Mackey says, 'one other gift the pundits share is a frighteningly accurate card-memory. This amounts practically to total recall . . . a discussion between two bridge addicts sounds rather like a dialogue between two electronic computers. . . .' Could it have something to do with patterns?

Trying to assess my own brain, and looking back on my early years, I can see now I was born with a strange mixture of cleverness and dumbness. I was smart at school and clever at exams, but I was very unobservant, often did not see what was right in front of my nose, tended to do what people told me, to be pushed around, to be too willing. My father used to bore my relatives by telling them 'how clever Joyce was' (I often wondered why they disliked me so), but my husband used to say that there could be a pink elephant in our front garden and I would not notice it. This 'dumbness' or lack of noticing and assessing the situation quickly has been a great disadvantage to me in learning bridge. It has taken me years to recognise that a psychic (phoney) bid has taken place. I used to keep wondering why so many points were turning up in my partner's hand! And I still fail to understand the implications of certain bidding sequences and card plays. I certainly do not have a bridge brain.

I have heard this type of brain described as 'a man's brain', but could that be because it is mostly observed in men, as the women with it are often helping their children with their homework? How my heart warmed to those men who made a point of expressing their view that there was no difference between the male and female brain. And nearly 30 years ago, Guy Ramsey in *Aces All*[16] said 'bridge is not a game wherein physical strength, or even physical stamina, seems a cardinal requisite. The mind of woman, I still hold, is fully the equal of that of a man. But as a realist I am compelled to confess that a quartet of girls will, usually, fail against four chaps . . . perhaps they are subconsciously overawed by the traditional superiority of the male sex to "The Ladies—God bless 'em"; . . . possibly their judgment is, from centuries of being

59

forbidden (by men) to exercise it on theoretical subjects, not quite so practised as that of men. . . .'

To return to those who gave contradictory views. A small percentage of men said that men play better bridge because they have more flair. The same percentage said women have more flair. Similar statistics emerged saying women do not succeed because they do not show enough discipline, do not work on their systems enough, while others said they were too disciplined, 'too faithful to routine'; 'stick to the system too much'. These are small numbers in a large sample, but they indicate that men are confused about women, and this in turn leads to women's confusion about themselves. Given that women are expected to take their views from men, it leads to lack of confidence in themselves, a lack of perception about what they are and what they are to do. If they were confident in themselves, as men are, these expressed differences of opinion about them would not matter.

This is another case where I can see a perfect example in my life. Although there was never any thought that I would take over my father's business, I never quite divorced myself from it. I kept returning to it to 'help out' in the supportive role women occupy. Then, after my father's retirement, when the business was going very badly under a young manager he had appointed, my father asked me to return to 'keep an eye on things'. This I did, still in a supportive role, and being there full-time I soon found that far more was involved than mere bad management. The young man had to be dismissed. 'Well,' said my father, at this late stage in my life, 'you'd better run the business'. 'But I don't know enough,' I said. 'You can't do worse than what has been happening,' said my father. The strange thing was that once I sat in the Managing Director's chair, people treated me differently, and important information kept landing on my desk. Women tend to see themselves as men see them.

To return to the subject of women and flair it is interesting to examine the cases of Rixi Markus and Helen Sobel, put by all men among the women's greats. Both were said to have tremendous flair, to play intuitively. 'Doing things by intuition' is another excuse men use to deprive women of promotion. It is said to be too feminine and not reliable. If one studies the games of both Rixi and Helen, however, it is hard to sustain the argument that they played by intuition. It seems obvious that they both had the bridge brain mentioned earlier, and that their so-called intuitive bids and play came from solid logic and a knowledge of where the cards lay.

About the famous 'Rixi bids', Rixi herself writes, in *Bid Boldly, Play Safe*,[17] that 'risky they may be, but the risk is always a calculated one. No doubt it is because they are made by a woman that their success has often been attributed to "intuition" and "flair"—or even to hypnotic powers. I have no patience with such nonsense. Bridge is not an occult art; it is a game of intellectual skill—and luck . . . victory must be earned by . . . logical analysis.' In that same book, Albert Morehead wrote, 'I have seen quite a few Rixi bids that were unfathomable to me at the time. But later, either when Rixi explained them or when I took time to analyse them, I discovered they were based in inexorable logic.'

In another book, *Commonsense Bridge*[18] Rixi writes that as early as the age of four she used to watch her father and friends play cards, and 'was soon aware I might play it better than they did'. An arrogant assertion no doubt, but proved when as only a teenager she was hailed as a 'bridge prodigy' and in Vienna 'professors and famous intellectual men' stood around and watched her play. She soon began to have successes in tournaments with Dr Hirschler. In order to stay in Vienna and play bridge she married at 19 a man much older than she was. The marriage was not successful and Rixi was seriously ill during a pregnancy, but when she returned to bridge Dr Paul Stern quickly persuaded her to join the Austrian Ladies Team. Then began her phenomenal run of successes,

61

in women's and open bridge, in Austria and in England. She was undoubtedly the possessor of a top bridge brain.

The same goes for Helen Sobel. In *Championship Bridge* by J. Patrick Dunne and Albert A. Ostrow[19] one reads that 'it has been said more than once that Helen plays by ear, a statement which may be construed to mean . . . she relies exclusively upon so-called feminine intuition'. But the authors continue: 'Don't let anybody tell you that Helen Sobel is not a first-rate technician. I've never seen her make the wrong percentage play for a situation, and that despite the fact that she may pretend she's a lousy mathematician'. And later, 'nearly all women have some characteristic that betrays them under strain. Not Helen . . . what stamina!' Many women with keen brains, and Helen would appear to have belonged to this category, assume a 'dumb blonde' or feminine 'play by intuition' stance. They have been taught to do this to attract men. At the Casino at Biarritz I saw a woman bridge player, who had just covered herself with glory at the bridge table, pretending she did not know how to play Blackjack and appealing to the men for advice. The reason for this type of attention-seeking behaviour is because women get conflicting messages about what appeals to men.

Many men do not know what they want of women. They want them to be pure and virgin in their behaviour but sexy in bed. They want them to be weak and dependent as wives but strong and untiring as mothers. They want them to be mentally inferior, not to challenge men's superiority in games of skill, but intelligent enough to rear children and survive on their own when left at home. If told often enough they are illogical, or too emotional, or given enough conflicting messages about how they should behave, then women become confused and do become inferior people, seeking refuge in tears and weakness, opting out in difficult situations.

Perhaps we could return to that well-known bridge writer who is quoted at the head of this chapter and see how logical he is. As well as saying that most women are 'remarkably illogical', he said 'men do everything better. They play better chess, they are better artists, architects, abortionists, engineers, lawyers, bankers, rabble-rousers, politicians, crooks . . . even in domains which have been the preserves of women from time immemorial it is the men who have excelled. The Bayeux tapestry was woven by men. The best chefs are men.' What is meant here is not that men are *better*, but because they can stay in the workforce, they reach the top professionally. 'Having made this point,' he continued, 'may I say that I far prefer women to men and place them higher in the scheme of things. Of course sex has had a lot to do with it, but it is not the only factor. Women have charm and a better sense than have men at putting first things first. A man makes money. A woman makes the home, the only source of lasting happiness. The man provides the means, the woman ensures the end. Feminists do their sex a very poor service by trying to rob it of its main asset, femininity. Why should women play men at their game, when their own is so much better?'

This is an illogical statement. If men are better at everything, how is it women are better at making a home? Also, if they *are* better at making a home, it is only because that is what most of them see as their top priority. If more men spent more time on home-making, maybe they would be better at it than women. It is also illogical to say that women have 'a better sense than have men at putting first things first'. Making a good home is only seen by women as better because that is how men see women as best employed. It is very comfortable and comforting for men to have women at home caring for all their physical and emotional needs. If men honestly believed it was a better way to spend their lives, they would be demanding a share of it. The truth is that men believe the better way is earning money, being successful in business or the professions, or winning at bridge. Which leads us to Omar Sharif.

CHAPTER 9

'Women are Much More Intelligent'

In his book, Omar Sharif says 'women are much more intelligent. The proof? You will never find them devoting all their time and energy to mastering so trivial a subject as bridge. They are content to play like a bird. So how can you expect them to play as well as men?'[20] This is an echo of the male remarks discussed at the end of the previous chapter. It is also a view that is supported by many of the other respondents, male and female.

There is a general feeling that women are playing a much more important part in life than merely being good at bridge: 'women place bridge in better perspective'; 'thank goodness . . . rarely do their priorities alter . . . men can be competitive to the exclusion of everything else'; 'women have to be more well-rounded, to manage a household'; 'a woman's inner sense of values tells her that bridge is not really a matter of life or death, but a man, whose ego is at stake, is a much harder fighter and treats bridge as a challenge to his mentality'; 'women's interests tend to be broader'; 'maybe there are less top women because they have a broader mind with more sound interests in art and society. Who can blame them?' Many other similar quotes from other men were given in the earlier chapter on women having fewer opportunities.

Some women echoed these sentiments: 'women have better things to do with their lives. Men do nothing else since student days. Women with brilliant minds, powers of

64

concentration, great energy, are either running a home, a business, or doing something creative and stimulating'; 'women have to be more versatile and usually do a few worthwhile things along the way'; 'what an asinine way to live', said Dorothy Truscott, about men's concentration on bridge.

This is one of those myths that do not stand the test of examination. It is true women have to become adept at a wide range of activities, to run a house and bring up children, but the real result is that they become expert at none. The above statements sound fine, and one glows to be a woman, but in real life this all-round ability brings no material rewards and the skills acquired are constantly downgraded. There are no medals for being an expert and devoted wife and mother, except in one's own eyes and hopefully in the eyes of one's husband and children, and sadly not always even there.

This supposedly superior being is generally looked upon as 'just a housewife'; she 'doesn't work'; her opinions are not listened or paid attention to; she is 'too emotional'; 'remarkably illogical'; she 'lacks judgment'. Women occupy the lowest and worst-paid jobs in the workforce (even with equal pay); at all stages they drop out of education at a younger age; in business they are not promoted or sent to training courses in case they get pregnant; they are told they talk too much, but are granted only about a quarter of the time in any serious discussions (surveys have proved this); while men go here and there on business, enjoy expensive business lunches and drive large cars, women stay home, care for the children and drive small secondhand cars; when, as a result of at its best a shared act of sex, women become unwillingly pregnant, many people discourage them from controlling their own bodies and having an abortion; large numbers of them are regularly assaulted by their husbands, and if they leave them they live in terrible poverty.

In effect, they are not superior, all-round beings. They lack power and decision-making ability. Most of them are second-class citizens, just as most of them are second-class bridge players. Is 'their game' better than that of men, if it places them at the bottom of the ladder? Is it 'intelligent' of them, as Sharif says, to allow themselves to be relegated to an inferior position in all areas of life as well as such a 'trivial' one as bridge? It is not treated as 'trivial' by men. They spend far more time on it than women do, but it suits them to pretend it is trivial and urge their wives to devote themselves to the altruistic matters of life.

And what if some women happen to want to excel in that trivial activity?

If one needed further proof that men do not truly consider women as better, superior people, one only has to read some of the comments made by respondents when they answered the question why most non-playing captains of women's teams were men. They paint a very unattractive picture of women. Strangely enough it was some of the same men who made these derogatory remarks who then maintained women were better people. There were, of course, many exceptions. One was Frank Stewart from the US. 'I don't see a male captain,' he said, 'contrived as a father figure to give the team unity. And certainly not to separate the girls if any hair-pulling occurs.' It was another of those replies which warmed one's heart. Unfortunately, there were many men and women who did not agree with him, as shown in Table 12.

Some of the comments accompanying the replies give a revealing picture of how some men see women, and how some women see themselves. For example, from the men: 'women do not relate well to other women. There is more dissension in women's teams, and men can smooth things over. At work, women do not like working for other women'; 'there is bickering and jealousy among women, so a man captain is needed'; 'women say women's bridge is nastier, men are more soothing'; 'there is less bitterness with a man . . . he needs the

66

TABLE 12

	Men who replied	Women who replied
Men have more experience, are better players	26.66%	25.39%
Men have more authority, father figure. Women defer to them	25.45%	22.22%
Men are better at solving jealousy and ill-feeling among women	21.21%	9.52%
Women prefer a man	19.39%	22.22%
Jobs for the boys (said in many ways)	12.12%	4.76%
All the good women are already in teams	3.63%	11.11%
There *are* many good women captains	4.24%	15.87%
Don't know, no good reason	7.27%	6.34%
Times are changing and will change more	6.06%	6.34%
Women do not have the time	—	14.28%
Do resent the fact	—	14.28%
Women are more caring	—	4.76%

wisdom of Solomon, the patience of Job and the courage of a Sicilian judge'; 'men are brought up not to show emotions. There is more jealousy in a women's team. Women trust men more'; 'more in-fighting'; 'more traumas and disagreements'; 'six women together in such an ego game as bridge is bad enough—seven would be impossible'; 'women always prefer a man as a boss'; 'women are jealous'; 'men have much better control over a bunch of ladies'; 'there is too much emotion already with six women. It would be worse with the seventh';

'women do not like taking orders from other women'; 'men are more capable of keeping a group of temperamental females under control'; 'men are peacemakers'; 'the job needs stoicism, inspiration and authority, rarely found in women. Besides what six women would ever agree on a woman captain?'; 'women tend to be bitchy with each other and need a man'; 'administrators feel women become involved in petty disputes and clashes of personalities. *I do not hold this view*'; 'women in general do not like women as superiors'; 'curiously enough, the women in a team are more amenable to the discipline of a man and much less bickering occurs. A wench is a wench, after all, for which thank God.'

Very emotive, some of these comments. Unfortunately, some of the women agree. 'Women lose their heads in a crisis, and take advice better from men'; 'women don't take criticism from women, they don't think they are good enough, they respect men's tact and ability more, they are not jealous of men'; 'women still don't respect other women. There is too much jealousy'; 'only women in a team is a catastrophe'; 'you don't want a bunch of women together at a banquet'. These were the only actually derogatory comments received from women. Mostly, when they said they preferred men, it was because the men had more experience and were better players. Several of them said they themselves did not have time, 'leave it to the men'. Several said they found women captains better. Said one woman: 'we have a woman captain this year. It is nice. She is so comforting and easier to discuss things with. We have always had a man before, but this year we have a marvellous woman'.

No doubt there is 'bickering' in some women's teams, just as there are 'arguments' in some men's teams. The male comments quoted above seem to reinforce the view that men *notice* when women behave badly more than when women behave well. It is similar to when a woman is labelled 'aggressive' when all she has done is express a view, in ever so

68

mild a voice, different from that held by men. It is seen as *strength* in a man if he stands up for himself and has a good argument. To dissent is seen as a *weakness* in women. All the wonderfully supportive attitudes that women have to each other, in teams and partnerships, are completely overlooked. Women are much more likely to say 'it does not matter' or 'don't worry' when their partner makes a mistake. It is possibly even a *fault* of women's bridge, one of the reasons they do not succeed as much. Many of the men themselves have given evidence of how much more 'pleasant' and 'amenable' women are as partners.

In regard to women not liking a woman boss, I have been a woman boss for 15 years, with an almost completely female staff, and I have never lost one good employee except to a better job (in a small business it is difficult to give deserved promotion to very good young women) or to motherhood. I am not unique. Women bosses generally tend to be more caring and considerate, less unrealistic and unreasonable.

The comments about women and non-playing captains support the view that many women perceive themselves as men perceive them. It is not only what men say about such subjects as women's bridge, but the general overall picture women receive from advertising, religion, the media and other opinion leaders, a picture of women as non-competitive and non-aggressive people, content to fulfil the happy role of home-makers. It is men who are behind those messages, men who dominate the media, big business, politics and the church.

Not only are the messages about their behaviour such as to make them under-achievers, they are also conflicting. Women are seen as bitchy and eye-scratching, but also pleasant and amicable. It is part of what I call 'the door-opening syndrome', another classic way men keep women in their place. When discussing feminism with men, they frequently ask, 'but don't you want to have the door opened

69

for you?' To which I reply, hopefully quite nicely, 'Well, actually I quite like opening doors. I would much rather a man had scrubbed the floors for me or changed the babies' nappies'. Men pretend they put women on pedestals, but when it comes to the basic things of life, they allow women to do all the worst jobs. In factories, women have the worst, lowest paid jobs, and in the home they are left with all the dirty, soul-destroying tasks. All this is justified by many men because they open a few doors, or give a woman a part of their pay packet. This, in most cases, goes to buying food for the family and clothes for the children, but not much for the woman.

So, in bridge, women are to be satisfied with poor results, while men tell them how good they are as dependent mothers and wives.

CHAPTER 10

Bridge is Different

When I started writing this book, I had decided that the small number of women among the top bridge players around the world reflected the situation of women in most realms of human endeavour. Factors such as socialisation and male attitudes were just as relevant in bridge as in business, the professions or politics. I also believed that the really top women were probably not as good as the very top men. They were no longer winning open pairs, and they seldom took part in top open teams events in international competitions. The same reasons caused this, too many roles to play, too much the need to be a 'superwoman', and too many negative influences in early upbringing.

This however, is *not* a reflection of society in general, for in other areas one does regularly find women at the top. Why then is top bridge almost completely dominated by men? In a game of cerebral as against physical skill why do men win all the top competitions? The more I thought about it, the more I tabulated and studied both the statistics and comments I had collected, the more I changed my thinking. I have now decided that probably the top women players are as good as the top men. Many of those who replied to the questionnaire believe this. 'They play like a man'. One finds women in European, Asian and Australian international teams. Norma Borin was in the Australian open team for the Olympiads on the two occasions when it gained its best results with third

71

placings. She has the third largest number of masterpoints in Australia, and has twice won the McCutcheon Tropy, for the most masterpoints in one year in Australia. Mary McMahon was in the Australian team when it won the Far Eastern Open Championship in 1970. In 1984, Linda Peterson in the US was beaten in only the last few weeks for the McKenny Trophy and both she and Ron Anderson (the winner) broke the previous record for points by a large margin. Barbara Travis (Gill) was the youngest ever Grand Master in Australia. Many women have played in European open teams.

So women are competing and winning near the top. But they seem either not quite to get there or to be going slowly backwards. As far as I can trace there has never been a woman in an open team that came first or second in the European championships. In the US, probably recognised as the strongest bridge nation at the moment, it is some time since there has been a woman in their open international teams. In the Bermuda Bowl World Championships Josephine Culbertson and Helen Sobel were in the US team that came second in 1937. Dorothy Hayden Truscott was in the US team that came second in 1965. In the World Team Olympiads no women in any countries have appeared in winning teams.

So why is bridge different? One theory that began to emerge was that perhaps it is not women's lack of ability but the nature of the game, and three reasons have appeared to support this.

The first is that there is probably less room at the top in bridge. In contrast to any other sport or pastime (except chess) top people seem to stay there forever. There is no slow disappearance of champions to be gradually replaced by younger up-and-coming players. Study the American team for the 1984 Olympiad in Seattle. It is comprised of Malcolm Brachman-Ron Andersen, Bobby Wolff-Bob Hamman, and

Bobby Goldman-Paul Soloway. *The Contract Bridge Bulletin* (US) says 'Hamman-Wolff and Soloway-Goldman are, with one or two possible exceptions, the most experienced international players available to represent the ACBL. All are former members of the Aces Team put together by the late Ira Corn. As Hamman notes, "If you want to get down to cases, since 1969 there has been only one year that none of us was on the international team". (The exception was 1981.)

'Hamman will be appearing in world knockout team play for the 13th time. His first appearance was in the New York Olympiad in 1964. He won the world team title in 1970, 1971, 1977 and 1983. Wolff has won the same four world team championships as Hamman and will be representing the ACBL for the tenth time in international team play.

'Goldman won the world team title in 1970, 1971 and 1979. He will be representing the ACBL for the eighth time in knockout team championships. Soloway in seven previous appearances has won three world championship titles. His Bermuda Bowl championships came three in a row. He was on the team that deposed the Italians in Monte Carlo and also was first in Manila in 1977 and in Rio in 1979.' In other words these men *were at the top* 15 to 20 years ago.

The runners-up were Edgar Kaplan-Norman Kay, Jeff Meckstroth-Eric Rodwell and Richard Pavlicek-Bill Root. Only Meckstroth-Rodwell represent a younger generation, and what vast experience is found in both these teams. It is a very discouraging future for younger players, no matter how much promise they have. Only in golf do we see older men, such as Player and Nicklaus holding their places, and there are still new younger men regularly beating them. In bridge younger men have to devote ten to 20 years to aspire to the top and even then quite brilliant players do not make it. How much more difficult for women to break through.

In what other activity could the extraordinary feat of the late Oswald Jacoby be repeated. He was one of the participants in the very early days of bridge promotion. In 1931, in the 'Battle of the Century' he partnered Sidney Lenz in that greatly publicised match with Ely and Jo Culbertson to prove which system was the better. There was huge betting, razzamatazz and media attention. It continued for weeks and after the first 108 rubbers an argument between Lenz and Jacoby resulted in Jacoby withdrawing (who says it is only women who cannot get along with their partners?) Then, in late 1983, over 50 years later, he was in the winning team in the Reisinger in the Nationals at Miami, 'an unbelievable man' according to *The Bridge World* (August 1984), 'a dying man in his eighties, totally concentrated through gruelling 30-board and 32-board sessions of board-a-match, fighting every bit as fiercely as always, playing magnificently, and *enjoying it*.'

So it is not only the woman champions who have trouble getting to the top. If we compare bridge with politics, medicine, science or business, where we do find a few women at the top, the field is far wider. There are not ten top business people, for example, or ten top scientists. If there were, we would probably not find any women amongst them. There have been women Prime Ministers, but politics is not a measurable activity. Getting to the top depends on many unpredictable factors, the nature of one's own party, one's ability to manoeuvre and manipulate, the nature of one's opposition. All these apply to games, but not to the same extent. What many may see as the *best* politician, either male or female, often faces many obstacles to advancement to high places.

Further, in these other areas, compared to the physical areas of combat, there are not separate arenas for men and women. There is not 'women's politics' or 'women's medicine' or 'women's science'. To advance in these areas women must compete with men, and some of them ultimately achieve the higher places.

This leads to the very contentious subject of the existence of women's bridge as a separate competition at many levels, particularly at the top. This is the second way in which bridge is different. It is one of the few activities in the world where women can compete in the open events, equally with men, and can also compete in women's events. You can compete to represent Australia in the open teams, and you can also compete to represent Australia in the women's teams. Sometimes the events are held concurrently, so you have to decide in which section you will compete, but sometimes, as in Canberra at the beginning of each year, the women's trials take place first and are followed by the open. In the US similar patterns occur.

On the surface this gives women a great advantage. They have a double chance, and it is not surprising that men sometimes complain. They say women, who are assumed to be weaker, can lower the standard of the open, introduce more of a luck element, and then have their own events. At the same time, women complain at the increasing practice of holding both events together, which disadvantages women. They have to make a choice. As they usually choose the women's they are deprived of the tougher competition of the open. One can see both sides of this problem. That women have two chances is unfair to men, but it would be unfair to women to deprive them of competing in the open, and increase their tendency to choose the women's.

There have, over the years, been people who advocated, in order to improve women's bridge, that it should be abolished, and that everyone should compete in the open. David Askew and Ron Klinger in Australia have done this in print, and Norway, several years ago, did temporarily abolish women's bridge. The reactions from other people, particularly women, and other countries were definitely unfavourable. The answers to the questionnaire show that women seem to be universally against the idea (see Table 13), and who can

75

blame them? Through women's bridge, the top women players are able to win overseas trips and take part in international bridge. Given the difficulty of even the top men getting into open teams, women would find it extremely difficult to achieve success there, even if their bridge improved.

The majority of men are also against it, although many of them believe women's bridge would improve (see Table 14).

TABLE 13: SHOULD WOMEN'S BRIDGE BE ELIMINATED?

	Men who replied	Women who replied
No	78.18%	84.12%
Yes	16.36%	14.28%
No opinion	5.45%	1.58%

TABLE 14: IF SO, WOULD WOMEN'S BRIDGE IMPROVE?

	Men who replied	Women who replied
No	45.45%	53.96%
Yes	31.51%	22.22%
Possibly, probably, a little	16.96%	14.28%
No opinion	6.06%	9.52%

Most of the men gave as reasons that women preferred separate events and it gave them more chance to represent their country. Some said they should be eliminated ultimately, but not quite yet. Others had more selfish reasons and said women's events 'gave cheap masterpoints'; while others said it was not logical, as we do not have 'separate businesses for women', or 'different events for people with red hair', 'this is a cerebral event, so there should not be separate sections'. Others said there should not be women's and open but women's and men's events. Some said women's bridge at the top would improve but not at lower levels.

The women's replies showed a great agreement with the men's. Some women said in principle they agreed, but in practice it was very difficult to give up the chance for international trips, 'winning is fun'. Several also said it may mean some women would drop out, and others said women do prefer women's events. Several said they always played in the open anyway, and had played in open teams. Others said that they would like to try for the open teams ultimately, but would like to work towards it gradually. One woman said women's bridge was good enough already.

Both men and women expressed the view that as long as women continued playing women's bridge they would not be as good as men. 'They do not have to work as hard to get into the teams,' said one woman. 'Men's bridge is much tougher and more competitive,' said another. Jon Sveidal of Norway summed up this view very well: 'If women are to become better players they have to face the strongest possible competition, to go through the toughest possible training. Women's events are the goals many female players will regard as the ultimate goal, and to qualify they have to find female partners and play a lot in all-female qualifying events, in fields that don't give them the routine they need in open class.'

As already mentioned, Norway, because of this view, abolished women's teams. As this was not followed by other countries, and had the effect of merely disadvantaging Norwegian women, the decision was reversed.

If any further proof were needed of some men's true attitudes to women, not only in regard to bridge but in regard to character, it is shown in some of their comments made when answering these questions: 'No, because probably less women would compete'; 'no, men's bridge would deteriorate'; 'yes, but not as many would play'; 'would probably not improve but would eliminate women's bridge'; 'no, their bridge would get worse'; 'at the top yes, but there would be a falling off in others'; 'women would compete less frequently'; 'women's bridge would decline'; 'women would be discouraged'; 'it could eliminate women from top competition'; 'no, they keep women happy, and women are an important part of the game in many ways'; 'there would be too many women playing in the big events'; 'no, they brighten the scene. If all events became effectively men only, I would be most disappointed'; 'what would happen to the women?'; 'uneven fields are precarious enough'; 'women would give up, if no chance to win'; 'no, not until men stop mocking women'.

It is difficult to understand the view that women would be discouraged and drop out. After all, women are accustomed to being beaten by men, and at local congresses in Australia most of the events are open and men tend to dominate. This does not discourage the women, and from various replies the same seems to apply to other countries. But whatever the views for or against women's bridge, most agree that its separate existence weakens its standard. It is easier to win there, so women do not need to work as hard on their bridge, nor do they regularly face, at the top level, the tough, aggressive, competitive bridge played by top men. Finally, if they were forced always to play in the top open events, some women would surely ultimately succeed. It will be interesting to note the performance and progress of the top US women's team at present regularly competing in the open tennis events.

The third reason why bridge as a game is different is because I now believe that men's attitudes, far from being less discriminating than in other fields, are in effect more influential. Because of the structure of the game, the persistent belief by top men that women are not only less good at bridge but also, for various reasons, less acceptable as *partners* or as *members of teams* these days keeps women out of winning combinations. It would seem that until women's teams contest regularly in the open arena, and finally win themselves first places, they will be considered lesser players. But they will have to do it themselves. Generally speaking, and especially in the top echelons, men are not going to help them by any longer including them in top pairs and top teams, as shown in Tables 15 and 16.

TABLE 15: HAVE YOU CHANGED PARTNERS MUCH?

	Men who replied
Yes	29.69%
No	64.84%
No reply	5.45%

TABLE 16: HAVE YOU EVER CONSIDERED A WOMAN PARTNER FOR A TOP EVENT?

	Men who replied
Yes	56.96%
No	38.78%
No reply	4.24%

Several of the 'yes' replies were accompanied by remarks such as 'a disaster', 'never again' or 'with great success', 'considerable success', 'some success', or 'I always play with my wife', 'my regular partner is a woman'. It is interesting that many of the no answers to both questions were the top world players. Tables 17 and 18 give another example of male attitudes to women partners.

Comments made with the replies for these Tables included 'just for fun'; 'only for social bridge'; 'very pleasant and gracious events'; 'I hate them'; 'field too uneven'; 'not as good

	Men who replied
Yes	57.57%
No	42.42%

TABLE 18: DO YOU TAKE THEM SERIOUSLY?

	Men who replied
Yes	74.54%
No	24.24%
No reply	1.21%

standard'; 'a social event'; 'a gamble'. Some said they took all bridge seriously, and others that they took the mixed seriously 'but other men don't'. Some said they never played mixed, and others that their regular partner was their wife. Apart from those who played top class bridge regularly with their wives, often with excellent results, one can only deduce from these and other answers that top men generally do not today consider women partners as a serious proposition. If one examines the results of the 1982 World Championship at Biarritz, it is interesting to note the number of men who obtained good results with their wives or other women in the mixed, but had a male partner in the open, and mostly did not do as well.

The other side of the coin is that some women say they prefer women partners, and most of them say they have no problem getting partners, either male or female, as is shown in Tables 19, 20 and 21. The only problem here is that top women obviously no longer have top men as partners. This is possibly because, facing the male attitudes already set out, women are willing to play with another good woman, although she may not be the best player available. Top men on the other hand, will only settle for the best.

TABLE 19: DO YOU HAVE TROUBLE GETTING PARTNERS?

	Women who replied
No	73.01%
Yes	20.63%
No reply	6.34%

Comments covered other women getting pregnant, good partners being rare, preferring to play with different people, playing with husbands.

TABLE 20: DO YOU PLAY MUCH WITH MEN PARTNERS?

	Women who replied
Yes	76.19%
No	17.46%
No reply	6.34%

Those who never played with men included strong female pairs, who always played together. Others said they always played with men.

TABLE 21: HAVE YOU FOUND DIFFICULTY GETTING MEN PARTNERS?

	Women who replied
No	73.00%
Yes	20.63%
No reply	6.34%

Again, several said they played with their husbands; others that they preferred women; and some that they were prevented by jealous wives; while one said, (something I have noticed), that young men on the way up like to play with competent women, but 'ditch them later on for men'. Two also mentioned that although they could find plenty of male partners, they were not the top men, who preferred to play together.

So we return to the fact that if women in countries like the US, Australia, New Zealand, or the leading European countries, where the men have dominated the open for some time, want to achieve that position, they will probably have to do it with all-female teams. But why should they? They have several other goals to achieve first. Strong women's teams do not always win the women's trials. The winners change from year to year, so there is great effort required to attain the country's women's team. Then there is the goal, if one is in the team, of that team winning the international event. It will be interesting to notice the progress of the Dutch women's team. A great deal of money has been spent on training them in tough, competitive, aggressive, male bridge, and they were disappointed not to win the last European championship, but so much can go wrong in a bridge tournament. This reinforces the view it is not surprising women do not face the extra hurdle of events dominated by men.

CHAPTER 11

Ten Rules for Success

Perhaps a final look could be taken at what makes a good bridge player. When I first started playing seriously and had my first tuition from the Borins, Jim Borin told me three things were necessary:

1. To read about and study the game as much as possible;
2. To play as much as possible;
3. To kibitz leading players as much as possible.

Having carried out these instructions to the best of my ability, I then discovered there were additional factors. It became apparent there were other traits necessary, characteristics it was necessary to *have* as well as things I had to *do*. The additional factors were:

4. To be aggressive;
5. To be competitive;
6. To concentrate;
7. To be courageous;
8. To have confidence;
9. To have good judgment;
10. To have a good partner.

These ten requirements have been discussed in this book. For the first three one requires time and money. Women are disadvantaged here compared with men. For the next four, women are disadvantaged by their upbringing, how they are taught women should act and be. For the last three requirements they are disadvantaged by men's attitudes, how men judge them, how men make women see themselves. In bridge this is particularly damaging, not only because of the partnership and team angle, but because men describe bridge as only a 'game' or a 'pastime'. It is therefore particularly easy for them to rationalise women out of trying too hard, to use the argument that women are leading much better lives by concentrating on the home.

After all, if a woman is working hard and being successful in a business, a scientific, medical or political area, it is not so easy for men to persuade her that her particular field is 'unimportant' or 'trivial'. She knows differently. She knows it is of value, and that she is also earning good money from it. When it comes to a mere game of skill, it is different. It is much more difficult for a woman to justify neglecting her home and spending days, nights, weekends, even weeks on bridge, especially if her obsession costs rather than earns money.

Notes

1 Jessie Bernard, *The Future of Marriage*, Souvenir Press, London, 1972, pp. 33–34.

2 Omar Sharif, *Omar Sharif's Life in Bridge*, Faber, London, 1983, p. 22.

3 K. F. Dyer, *Challenging the Men*, University of Queensland Press, St Lucia and New York, pp. 73 and 98: 'To compensate for women's generally lower levels of muscular strength they have two important advantages: their endurance and flexibility are greater. The static muscle fatigue patterns of men and women are not significantly different (that is the amount of time which they can exert maximal muscular force). But women's relative endurance is better. Tests in which the subject sustains a submaximal force level at a set percentage of that individual's maximal voluntary contractile strength (MVC) show that in tests utilizing between a quarter and three quarters MVC women are superior. The superiority of women is greater at lower levels of MVC.' And, discussing the successes women are having in long distance events and the fact they are fast narrowing the gap between the times of women's and men's events, Dyer says it poses 'two questions. First, how much more potential is there among women, who are so consistently told that they have less potential than men anyway? Second, what unrecognized potential is there among women for events in which at present they do not often compete—the long distance events, steeplechase, walks and so on. The performances by women in events fairly new to them,

such as the marathon and the 400 metres hurdles, demonstrate quite conclusively that there is indeed a great deal of unexpressed potential among sportswomen.'

4 Ann Oakley, *Housewife*, Pelican, London, 1976, pp. 100–101. Oakley compares housework to factory work, particularly assembly line work, one of the lowest status work areas. The worst features of housework are similar to and actually worse than those of assembly line workers. Both experience monotony, fragmentation (work as a series of unconnected tasks, none of which require the worker's full attention), isolation, and excessive speed as a source of dissatisfaction as follows:

	Monotony	Fragmentation	Speed
Housewives	75%	90%	50%
Factory Workers	40%	70%	31%
Assembly Line Workers	67%	86%	36%

5 Ever since women started laying claim to equal opportunity with men, theorists have been trying to prove that either women's brains were different and/or inferior. Not only has no proof of this ever been produced, but the theories themselves have changed as one after another has been disproved. Feminists naturally claim that the putting forward of such claims is an attempt to keep women in their place.

Back in the nineteenth century, when women were fighting for equal education, it was firmly maintained that if women used their brains their wombs would 'dry up', and they would be of no use as mothers. This has obviously been proved wrong. Women are now earning top places in every discipline at university level, and those same women are producing fine, healthy children. Similarly, one of the arguments against giving women the vote was that they could not stand the roughness 'of the hustings'. Yet women were thrust into the dirt, squalor, and rigour of coal mines, factories, and scrubbing floors at home.

Readers wanting to read further will find detailed proofs

that there is no evidence whatsoever to show that women's brains are in any way different from those of men in the following:

Antony W. H. Buffery, 'Male and Female Brain Structure and Function: Neuro-psychological Analyses', and Lesley Rogers, 'Biology: Gender Differentiation and Sexual Variation', in *Australian Women: Feminine Perspectives*, Penguin 1981, Australia.

Also, Jeanette McGlone, 'Sex Differences in Human Brain Asymmetry: a Critical Survey', in *The Behavioural and Brain Sciences*, Cambridge University Press, 1980, and other articles in this magazine.

6 Pat Sheinwold, *Husbands and Other Men I've Played With*, Houghton Mifflin, Boston, 1976, pp. 52–55.

7 Ibid, p. 29.

8 Ibid, p. 34.

9 J. Patrick Dunne and Albert A. Ostrow, *Championship Bridge*, The Bodley Head, London, 1952, p. 21.

10 Henry G. Francis (ed.), *The Official Encyclopedia of Bridge*, Crown Publishing, New York, 1984, p. 755.

11 Dunne and Ostrow, p. 30.

12 *The Age*, Melbourne, September 3, 1984.

13 Ibid, September 7, 1984.

14 *The Age*, Melbourne, September 3, 1984.

15 Rex Mackey, *The Walk of the Oysters*, W. H. Allen, London, 1964, p. 159.

16 Guy Ramsey, *Aces All*, Museum Press, London, 1955, p. 100.

17 Rixi Markus, *Bid Boldly, Play Safe*, Bodley Head, London, 1966, p. 10.

18 Rixi Markus, *Commonsense Bridge*, Bodley Head, London, 1972, pp. 9–66.

19 Dunne and Ostrow, p. 111.

20 Omar Sharif, p. 80.

APPENDIX 1

The Questionnaires

QUESTIONNAIRE SENT TO MEN

1 List 3 or 4 of your main bridge achievements or activities.
2 How long have you been playing bridge?
3 How did you start?
4 What is your background and education?
5 What is your profession or work now?
6 Do you think men are more successful at bridge than women?
7 Give reasons for your answer.
8 If women were forced always to play open bridge, do you think they would improve?
9 Do you prefer playing bridge with a man partner rather than a woman?
10 Give reasons for your answer.
11 Why are women seldom selected in open teams?
12 Do you like mixed pairs competitions?
13 Do you take them seriously?
14 Should women's events be eliminated?
15 Why?
16 Would women's bridge improve if they were?
17 Have you changed partners much for important events?
18 Have you ever considered a woman partner for an important event?

19 If so, with what result?

20 Do you think men are ever sexually distracted by playing with or against women?

21 Do you think women are ever sexually distracted by playing with or against men?

22 Why do you think men are usually selected as non-playing bridge captains for women's bridge teams?

23 What system do you play?

24 Have you felt you have faced any obstacles in playing as much bridge as you would like?

25 Any other?

QUESTIONNAIRE SENT TO WOMEN

1 List 3 or 4 of your main bridge achievements or activities.

2 How long have you been playing bridge?

3 How did you start?

4 What is your home background?

5 What is your education? Your work training? Your profession?

6 Do you use or follow the above now?

7 Are you married?

8 Do you have any children?

9 Do you have help in the house?

10 Does your husband (if any) play bridge?

11 What is or was his attitude to your bridge?

12 Do you have any money problems with bridge?

13 Do you think men are more successful at bridge than women?

14 Give reasons for your answer.

15 Do you have trouble getting satisfactory partners?

16 Do you often play in competitions with men partners?

17 If not, would you like to play bridge more with men?

90

18 Have you found difficulty in doing the above?
19 Are women disadvantaged officially in any way in your country?
20 Do you often play in open events?
21 Do you play in any particular type of open event?
22 Do you ever choose open events instead of women's?
23 If so, why?
24 Should women's events be dropped?
25 Would that improve women's bridge?
26 Do you feel men are ever sexually distracted by playing with or against women?
27 Do you feel women are ever sexually distracted by playing with or against men?
28 What system do you play?
29 Why do you think non-playing captains of women's teams are usually men?
30 Do you resent the above?
31 Do you feel any obstacles, other than those already mentioned, have prevented you playing as much bridge as you would have liked?
32 Any other?

APPENDIX II

Men who Replied to Questionnaire

AARONSON, Lou   USA
ACHTERBERG, W.   Switzerland
AGARWALA, S. A.   India
ALDER, Phillip   UK
ARMANNSSON, Jakob   Iceland
ASKEW, David   Australia
ASHAY, S. Bertram   Canada
AUKEN, Jens   Denmark
BABSCH, Fritz   Austria
BARBONE, Guido   Italy
BECKER, B. Jay   USA
BECKER, Michael M.   USA
BECKER, Steve   USA
BELL, Bruce C.   New Zealand
BELLADONNA, Giorgio   Italy
BESSE, Jean   Switzerland
BIGAT, M. Halit   Switzerland
BIRMAN, David   Israel
BOEKHORST, A.   Holland
BOER, K. A.   Holland
BONOMI, Robert F.   USA
BORHO, Volker   West Germany
BORRE, J. van den   Belgium
BROWN, David   UK
BRUSZTUNOV, Vitold   USSR
CABANNE, Carlos   Argentina
CAMPBELL, Henry   France
CARRUTHERS, John   Canada
CHAGAS, Gabriel P.   Brazil
COPELAND, Allan J.   USA
CORNELL, Michael   New Zealand
COTTER, E. P. C.   UK
COURT, R. A.   Republic of South Africa

CUMMINGS, Dick   Australia
CUNNINGHAM, Howard   Canada
CUPPAIDGE, George   Australia
D'ORSI, Ernesto   Brazil
DAHL, Fleming   Denmark
DANAN, M. Charles   Morocco
DIMITRESCU, Dan   Romania
DUCHEYNE, Rene   Holland
ETTLINGER, D. M.   Republic of South Africa
EZEKIEL, David   Bermuda
FALK, Allan   USA
FELDMAN, Ron   USA
FLEET, R. J.   UK
FLODQUIST, Sven-Olov   Sweden
FOX, G. C. H.   UK
FRANCIS, Henry   USA
FRANCOS, Luis   Spain
FRASER, Douglas   Canada
FRENDO, Paul   Italy
FREY, Richard L.   USA
FURUSETH, Magne   Norway
GAROZZO, Benito   Italy
GAUTHIER, Maurice   Canada
GHOSE, Santanu   India
GIBSON, Tom   Ireland
GIMKIEWICZ, Benno   Thailand
GOKHALE, M. R.   India
GOODWIN, Thomas L.   USA
GOSLING, A. R.   UK
GRENSIDE, Richard William   Australia
HAAGENSEN, Sverre   Norway
HAGEMAN, J. J. H.   Holland
HAGLUND, Per   Sweden

93

HALLEN, Hans-Olof   Sweden
HELMAN, Leonard A.   USA
HEYN, Dr. Med. W.   West Germany
HOFFMAN, Martin J.   UK
HUTCHINSON, David G.   USA
JACKSON, David   Ireland
JACOBY, James O.   USA
JAMIESON, Peter   Australia
JOHNSON, Jared   USA
JUFFERMANS, Pim   Holland
KANTAR, Eddie   USA
KANTAR, Nicu   Romania
KAPLAN, Edgar   USA
KEHELA, S. R.   Canada
KLEWE, W. E.   UK
KLINGER, Ron   Australia
KNIGHT, John   New Zealand
KOKISH, Eric   Canada
KUROKAWA, Akio   Japan
LAROCHELLE, Maurice   Canada
LAVINGS, Paul   Australia
LERCH, Armin   Belgium
LESTER, John   Australia
LEUICK, Richard A.   USA
LEVINREW, George E.   Israel
LIEN, Reidar   Norway
LOURENTZ, Donald A. L.   UK
LUNDBY, I. B.   Denmark
MACCRACKEN, Charles M.   USA
McNEIL, Keith   Australia
MARSTON, Paul   Australia
MARSTRANDER, Peter   Norway
MILNES, Eric   UK
MOELLER, Steen   Denmark
MOLLO, Victor   UK
MORE, Hal de   USA
MORTENSEN, Tore   Norway
MUGFORD, Gary   Canada
MUSUMECI, Joe   USA
NEAMTZU, Coriolan   Romania
NEY, Marcel Francois   Republic of
   South Africa
NIKITINE, Nick   Switzerland
NORTH, Freddie   UK
NOVRUP, Svend   Denmark
O'KEEFFE, John H.   Ireland
OONG, Gim C.   Canada
OPSTAD, Emil   Norway

ORTIZ-PATINO, J.   France
OUDSHOORN, Nico D.   Holland
PECHE, George   Ireland
PENCHARZ, W. J. (Bill)   UK
PHAF, William M. J. C.   Holland
PIGOT, Peter   Ireland
POWLEY, J. S. (Jay)   Canada
PRESSBURGER, Dr John   West
   Germany
RACOVICEANU, Vlad H.   Romania
REBATTU, M. J.   Holland
REESE, T. J.   UK
REX-TAYLOR, D.   UK
RIMINGTON, Derek   UK
ROBINSON, Arthur Guy   USA
ROSENKRANZ, Dr George   Mexico
ROWLAND, V. M.   New Zealand
RUBENS, Jeff   USA
RUMMELL, Dirik, Baron von
   West Germany
SACHEN, Bill   USA
SALAMA, Freddy   France
SALGO, Gabor   Hungary
SCHAPIRO, Boris   UK
SCHERER, Harold   UK
SCHIPPERHEYN, Ton   Holland
SCHROEDER, Dirk   West Germany
SHARMA, Col. V. S. M.   India
SHEINWOLD, Alfred   USA
SHENKIN, Barnet J.   UK
SIMON, John E.   USA
SMILIE, Henry   Canada
STABELL, Leif-Erik   Norway
STALLARD, Berl   USA
STEWART, Frank   USA
STOVER, Mel   Canada
STRONG, Tom   Australia
SVEINDAL, Jon   Norway
TARLO, Joel   Spain
THIBAULT, Gaitau   Canada
THORPE, Jerry   USA
TOMEK, Dr Vladimir   Ireland
TRIPPETT, Bernard   USA
TRUSCOTT, Alan   USA
VILLANYI, Dr Agoston   Hungary
WATKINS, D.   Australia
WAHLGREN, Anders   Sweden
WALSH, Patrick F.   Ireland

94

WEISS, Larry   USA
WEISZ, Harry   USA
WHITEBROOK, Chas.   USA

WITTERS, J. M. ('Jos')   Holland
WOODWORTH, R. M.   USA
ZAMZAMI, Amran   Indonesia

Women who Replied to Questionnaire

ARNESEN, Kirsten Rita   Norway
BACK, Patricia Margaret   Australia
BAMBERGER, Gabriele   Austria
BERRY, Dolores A.   USA
BOARDMAN, Kathy   New Zealand
BURNS, Bess   Canada
CALDWELL, Bobbye J.   USA
CHODOROWSTA, Irena   Poland
COOK, Jerry   USA
CORMACK, Jan   New Zealand
CUMMINGS, Val   Australia
DAVIS, Anita 'Pidgeon'   USA
DUCHEYNE, Elly   Holland
EVITT, Jane   New Zealand
FLEMING, Irene (Dimmie)   UK
FRASER, Sandra   Canada
GANNON, Elva   Ireland
GOKHALE, Sulabha A.   India
GOTHE, Eva-Liss   Sweden
GRIGGS, Eloene T.   USA
HARRISON, Ruth   USA
HAVAS, Elizabeth   Australia
HEATH-LATIMER, Mickey   USA
HEIMBUCK, Carolyn   USA
HELM, Emmy van der   Holland
HORTON, Sally   UK
HULGARD, Lida   Denmark
HUUN, Sigrid   Norway
HYATT, Irene   USA
JACOBSON, Rita   Republic of
   South Africa
KAAS, Petra   Holland

KANE, Tess   Ireland
KAPLAN, Betty   USA
KOPPANG, Annelise   Norway
LAFOND, Yvonne   Canada
LANDY, Sandra   UK
LEDERER, Rhoda   UK
LUSK, Susan   Australia
LUX III, Mrs Samuel E.   USA
MCLAUGHLIN, Stella   Australia
MALLANDER, Antha   USA
MARKUS, Rixi, MBE   UK
MATTHEWS, Lillian   Spain
MENG, Gloria   Taipei
MIYAISHI, Etsuko   Japan
MOELLER, Kirsten   Denmark
MOSES, Kinga   Australia
ODLUND, Britt-Marie   Sweden
OKKERSE, Anke   Holland
RADIN, Judy   USA
RUPPERT, Greta   USA
SCHIPPERS, Elly   Holland
SCHROEDER, Louise   USA
SITHI-SARIPUTRA, Boonita   Thailand
SOPHONPANICH, Esther   Thailand
STAVELEY, Anne   UK
STERN, Gerda   Australia
SUPARTO, Nette   Indonesia
TOUBES, Judith   USA
TRAVIS, Barbara   Australia
TRUSCOTT, Dorothy Hayden   USA
VALENSI, Odile   France
WEI, Katherine   USA